BEAR

VS.

MAN

BEAR

RECENT ATTACKS AND HOW TO
AVOID THE INCREASING DANGER

BY BRAD GARFIELD

Willow Creek
P R E S S

VS. MAN

ACKNOWLEDGMENTS

From the beginning, my supportive wife, Maureen, has stood by my side, understanding the long hours locked in my office, patiently waiting for the phone line to clear, and understanding the days and sometimes months I spend chasing animals with a camera. Without her, this book would have been impossible. She has always been my rock — anchored to a cheerful attitude, willing to help in any way she can, and reluctantly yet encouragingly seeing me out the door with a hug and shove. Thank you, Maureen, for always being there when I need you.

There is no way I can possibly repay my parents, J.R. and Judy Garfield. They have always been there. It seems inadequate but all I can say is thank you. I couldn't have asked for a better influence on my life.

Thank you, Kim, you are a true friend.

I would like to thank Tom Smith. His help answering my pages of e-mails has enlightened me and provoked me to provide the answers to hard questions. His experience and expertise are greatly appreciated.

There are too many individual people to thank. If I tried, I am sure I would miss someone who contributed in any way to this book. To everyone, I simply say thank you.

—B.G.

© 2001 Brad Garfield

Photo Credits: Photos copyright Brad Garfield except as otherwise noted.

Published by Willow Creek Press, P.O. Box 147, Minocqua, Wisconsin 54548

Design by Patricia Bickner Linder
Edited by Andrea K. Donner

For information on other Willow Creek Press titles, call 1-800-850-9453

Library of Congress Cataloging-in-Publication Data
    Garfield, Brad
       Bear vs. Man : recent attacks and how to avoid the increasing danger / Brad Garfield.
          p. cm.
       ISBN 1-57223-396-6 (softcover : alk. paper)
       1. Bear attacks.   I. Title.
       QL737.C27 G37 2001
       599.78'1566--dc21   00-012790

Printed in Canada

CONTENTS

INTRODUCTION

My hometown's mascot is the bear. At the entrance to the local high school, a weathered bronze statue of a black bear stands frozen, nose in the air as if sniffing the wind for prey. It is a powerful figure, an image we as teenagers hoped would send fear into our rivals as they entered our territory, letting them know they entered at their own risk. It may not have, yet we were still proud to be called the "Bear River Bears." Years later, the bear still holds that power over me.

Tucked safely away in northern Utah, my formative years were spent hiking and exploring the lower canyons and valleys of the Rocky Mountains. Life was simple. My basic desire was to surround myself with new scenery and, if I was lucky, maybe see some critters along the way. I was raised in a family who enjoyed basically anything outdoors. For two weeks each summer we traveled elbow to elbow, cramped in a loaded-down station wagon, driving through national parks and camping in well-known tourist traps. Whether I was glued to a television watching Mutual of Omaha's *Wild Kingdom* or looking out the window of the family car scanning for likely animal hideouts, I just wanted to see animals.

During one of those family vacations, the car came to a halt. I was poised for action, ready to spring out the door, stopping only when my mother gave me a stern look that said, "stay in the car." In the distance, I spotted a black speck moving slowly through the meadow, apparently intent on making it to the treeline before anyone could see it. I reached for my newly-purchased, two-power, pop-up binoculars and squinted, straining hard to see though the less-than-stellar glass.

"What is it?" someone yelled.

"I think it's a bear," I replied, "but I'm not sure. Quit bumping me so I can get a better look!"

The next second, a fight to the death ensued when my myopic big brother grabbed the binoculars and refused to give them back. I'd had my turn and even though they were mine, apparently he'd decided he wanted to use them. The spot moved into the trees and the car pulled forward. I stared back hoping for another glimpse, but to no avail. It was to be my first definite unconfirmed bear sighting.

As I got older, I read anything I could find on bears, their behavior, and especially, about attacks. I was fascinated by these creatures that could take a man's head off with a flick of a powerful paw, yet would usually run at the faintest scent of a human. Some of the books were disturbing, but they all made the same point. Bears, at times, can be deadly.

In May of 1992, I was able to fulfill a lifelong dream. I loaded my Toyota 4-wheel-drive pickup with enough food for three months, said my good-byes, and embarked on a journey of discovery. I drove through Glacier, Waterton, Banff, Jasper and Kluane national parks and several other smaller, out-of-the-way state parks along the famous Alaskan Highway. My destination was Alaska's Denali National Park where my friend, Mike Francis (a well-known photographer), and I would spend

two weeks on a rarely-traveled gravel road that winds deep into the backcountry. Denali is noted for its large population of grizzly bears and stunning scenery. It is also home to the glacier-covered Mt. McKinley, North America's highest mountain at 20,320 feet above sea level. I had driven over 3,500 miles to reach the park and she did not disappoint me. Our first day we encountered a bear.

"Get in the camper," Mike yelled. "He's coming around the truck!"

Just as the truck door shut, the 400-pound grizzly came

BEAR VS. MAN
10

lumbering around the corner only feet away. The sound startled him for a moment but he moved closer and sniffed the door. His breath fogged the window as his face was only inches away. I promptly backed away from the window to the driver's side, hoping the extra distance would slow my heart beat. It didn't. I imagined how easy it would be for him to peel the door open or shatter the ⅛ inch of non-tempered glass which stood between him and me. Panic struck. Have you ever looked in a grizzly's face from less than a foot away? Their eyes are jet-black, expressionless, and seemingly lifeless. I could hear Mike saying something, but my heart was beating too loudly to understand him. The bear's fur was long and a blonde color. This coloration is sometimes referred to as a Toklat grizzly, a breed unique to the Denali area. Its well-defined muscles rippled as the bear paced back and forth at the door, apparently trying to decide what to do next. His basketball-sized head blocked my view as he looked away and then back at me; I tried to remember where I'd put the car keys. Suddenly his attention was elsewhere. Something I couldn't see was now more interesting than I was, and he took one step away and then another. He moved off a short distance and then turned back with a stern expression as if to say, "This is my house — stay in your room." I obeyed.

It was my first Alaskan grizzly experience and it proved to be a turning point in my life. The encounter left me with a deep appreciation for these magnificent animals. I had been allowed to enter its world and I instantly knew that I never wanted to leave it again. A fifty hour drive, 100-mile-long stretches of gravel, pot holes that could swallow a Volkswagen bug, and expensive gas and fast food were mentally and physically grueling, yet if I had not seen another bear on that trip, it still would have been a success.

As it turned out, it was a good year to see bears and we saw several along the road, photographing each that allowed us. With each bear came another story, but I will save them for another time.

———

I never thought of myself as a publisher, so when a college professor asked me to start a magazine, I was skeptical at first. However, as he talked, I thought, and before I knew it, I was immersed into the world of publishing. I did not know if it would work, but I knew one thing: I was passionate about bears. Maybe my passion could be used to enlighten more people.

I launched *Bears Magazine* with a credit card in the spring of 1995 and it hit the magazine stands with an enthusiastic audience. The magazine was filled with spectacular images but lacked support from some of the top bear scientists and biologists. They refused to give information at first, but as time went on and the magazine matured, they released tidbits of knowledge, helping it gain more and more credibility within the scientific community. News spread fast and subscriptions came in from around the globe. Suddenly, my job was to learn about bears and I loved it. I talked about bears with conservation groups. I spoke for hours on the phone to bear fanatics and enthusiasts, expanding my knowledge. As I talked and learned, my concern about their plight grew and I committed myself to helping bears in any way possible. The magazine was used for that purpose and it evolved to become a forum to educate the public about bears through stunning photography and informative text.

When I was asked to write this book, my first concern was the bear. The attacks discussed in this book are brutal and terrible, and the photographs are explicit, but if looked at objectively with the intent of learning from them, they can help us understand bears. I know from past experience that there is a fine line between sensationalism and truth. Bears are far from boring. It is easy to portray them as vicious, emotionless killers. However, as you read this book, it is my hope that it sparks a lifelong interest as well as a deep-rooted, unshakable respect for bears. It is my opinion that it is only through education about shrinking bear habitat and bears' instinctual behavior that we will be able to save these fascinating creatures.

Few people experience truly wild bears. I have been fortunate to experience several. My occupation and adventurous nature have taken me halfway around the world in search of bears and wild places yet unphotographed. For me, it is only in these wild places that adventures happen, around a bend of a high-country trail or landing a floatplane in some no-name alpine lake. My worst fear is to lose the wild in wilderness where humans can still feel scared and small. The grandness of these places, along with the incredible creatures that inhabit them, produce respect and awe in humans as we contemplate our place in the world, and our stewardship of the environment. Bears and humans will continue to meet as people encroach into wild places. We must learn to respect and understand bears' instincts in order to avoid tragic consequences for both people and bears.

WHY SOME BEARS ATTACK

The first Europeans to arrive on North American shores encountered bears. Early explorers like Lewis and Clark experienced "white bears," or grizzly bears. Their stories bring to life earlier days when odds were more evenly matched between humans and bears. Crude black powder weapons sometimes didn't work, misfiring as the settlers hunted the land for food. Bears were obviously more numerous then. An estimated 50,000 to 100,000 grizzly bears lived in a range from California to the Great Plains up until the nineteenth century.

Today, however, both bears and people are different. Civilization is devouring wilderness at an alarming rate. Prime bear habitat is being surrounded as man pushes his way deeper into the bear's living room, building homes and golf courses where bears once lived. Bears, especially grizzlies, do not like roommates, preferring a solitary existence. Sometimes, the bears aggressively push back, which usually brings swift judgment and the bear's demise by confident humans. High-powered rifles can dispatch hunted or "nuisance" bears quickly and efficiently from safe distances. But sometimes, when humans venture into bear habitat unarmed or unprepared, a bear will viciously attack and sometimes kill a person. In these attacks, the bears hold the upper hand as they are faster and stronger than humans, equipped with powerful jaws, razor-sharp teeth and claws, and immense size.

What triggers a bear to attack? Why does a bear run at the faintest scent, sight or sound of a human during one encounter, and charge a hiker from over 300 yards away at another time? Bears have been known to stalk humans as prey to be eaten. What makes them look at one human as a threat and another as potential prey? Fortunately, few people meet bears up close, even though an increasing number of hikers are strolling through the wilderness. When a bear does attack, however, it falls into one of the following types: predatory, provoked, and surprise.

TYPES OF BEARS

First, it is important to know the three types of bears that roam the North American continent. The black bear (*Ursus americanus*) is the most common, ranging from Alaska through Canada and south into the top two-thirds of the United States all the way from the Pacific to the Atlantic coast. It is smaller than the brown bear, and has a black or dark brown coat. The brown bear (*Ursus arctos*) is a large bear inhabiting western North America and northern Eurasia that has brown to yellowish fur, and the polar bear (*Ursus maritimus*) is a large white-furred bear living in Arctic regions.

The grizzly bear is a brown bear but it is considered a subspecies (*Ursus arctos* subsp. *horribilis*). A bear's location and diet determines whether it is called a brown bear (sometimes referred to as a coastal brown bear), or an "interior" grizzly. If you were to draw an imaginary line one hundred miles inland paralleling

Left, grizzly bear; right, brown bear. The brown bear inhabits western North America and Eurasia. Grizzly and Kodiak bears are both brown bears. Brown bears' fur coloration varies from chocolate-brown to golden and blonde.

The black bear is the most common bear in North America. It is smaller than the brown bear, and can have a deep black or dark, cinnamon-brown coat.

Though skilled hunters with incredible size and power, polar bears rarely attack humans, mainly because of their remote habitat.

Alaska's coastline, any bear (except black bears) living from the coast up to this border would be called a brown bear. The bears residing inland, inside the imaginary one-hundred mile border, would be called grizzlies. The Kodiak bear is also a brown bear that inhabits islands and coastal areas of Alaska (most notably Kodiak Island), and is sometimes considered a separate species (*Ursus middendorffi*).

Coastal brown bears are naturally larger than interior grizzlies because of location, diet (they mainly eat fish), and thousands of years of big bears breeding with big bears — genetically speaking. Interior grizzlies live on roots, berries, grasses and the occasional carcass or trout they may find, thus their growth is more limited. Another critical food source for the interior grizzly is the whitebark pine cone which produces a pea-sized nut. Each fall, when grizzly bears are frantically feeding to build up fat reserves to get them through winter, they travel to higher country to search out red squirrel caches. These nut caches are an essential food source for grizzlies. Some experts believe that the nuts are responsible for 40 percent of the bears' winter fat layers and are important for fertility.

Tom Smith, a wildlife research ecologist with the USGS Alaska Biological Science Center, has amassed a database of over 460 human/bear encounters in Alaska. The report is a treasure trove of information for anyone interested in bears. The database contains 82 variables which range from species of bear to the fate of the person and bear involved.

According to Smith's database, brown and grizzly bears account for 82 percent of the attacks in Alaska, whereas black bears account for only 12 percent. Only 1 percent is polar bear inflicted while the remaining 5 percent of attacks are unidentified.

"Since we have approximately three times the black as brown/grizzly bears in Alaska, I can project that out and say, with some authority, that any brown/grizzly bear encountered in the wild is more than 20 times more likely to be involved in a confrontation with a human than a black bear. If we look at fatalities, it is much worse, in that brown bears are responsible for over 90 percent of them in this state."

Bears are naturally scared of humans. We are an "unknown" to them. Some experts believe in the "super bear" theory, which is that bears treat humans as they would a bigger, dominant bear, preferring to avoid an encounter that might cause injury.

Smith has a different explanation. "Why would a bear route around a person it could clearly defeat? I tell people that, in my mind, this is no different than if you or I were to walk a trail in South Africa and suddenly encounter a rock hyrax [an 8-pound relative of the elephant resembling a squirrel] with its little fangs clearly in view. Would we rush up and attempt to grab it, or kneel close to observe it? Likely not. With no previous experience, we'd be very cautious, not knowing if the little critter was going to rush over and chomp on our leg or turn around and spray us with some obnoxious scent. Do they carry rabies? Do they bite? Although we are clearly superior in size, strength and intelligence, we route around them, preferring not to learn the hard way that bad news can come in little packages. Why are bears any different? If bears knew what we knew, we'd be dead. But they don't, and as long as the unknown remains firmly in place, we are safe."

Jim Halfpenny, a well-respected scientist and educator with a background in mammalogy and ecology, has conducted wildlife research around the world and has studied bears extensively.

"Bears appear to avoid situations where they have to fight," Jim says. "Solitary animals that must feed themselves can't go around attacking everything. If they got into a fight, one injured paw could finish them off."

Coastal brown bears tend to be more social than grizzlies. They learn to alter their personal space and their attitude when in crowded situations, such as at streamsides during the salmon spawn. When a normally solitary bear that has a "comfort zone" of say, 50 feet, enters a high density population such as McNeil River in Alaska, its personal space and behavior has to change if it wants to concentrate on catching fish. The once solitary bear has to fish alongside other bigger and sometimes more aggressive bears. If he wants to build the necessary fat reserves

In high-density bear populations, such as at Brooks River Falls in Alaska during the salmon spawn, brown bears become less aggressive toward each other in order to concentrate on catching fish.

Unlike grizzly bears, whose diet consists mainly of roots, some carrion and seasonal foods like berries, a brown bear's diet consists mainly of fish. Sub-adult brown bears move away from the river where it is safer to eat their hard-earned catches. Larger, dominant bears would steal their fish from them.

to sustain him through a long winter, he needs to learn to associate with these bears. Fighting over territory and personal space causes minor wounds that, in the wild, can be deadly. Consequently, his comfort zone is forced to shrink to about 20 feet, depending on how often he is around other bears.

"What appears to dynamically alter a bear's personal space is the frequency and proximity of bear-bear contacts," states Smith. "High density bear situations have the effect of shrinking a bear's personal space." This behavior also applies to human-bear contact.

The more a bear comes in contact with people, the more habituated it becomes to humans. It is a bear's personal space or comfort zone that causes the major problem between bears and people. If a bear becomes comfortable in the presence of humans, it will allow a person to approach too close. The bear's natural fear wanes and the unknown — people — becomes customary, which creates a higher chance of a tragic encounter.

PREDATORY BEARS

The pursuit of food is a bear's foremost drive and will override any fear it has of humans if it's starving. Hungry bears can be edgy, nomadic, and troublesome. Each year, reports of black bears invading towns filter in across the nation. When bears become aggressive, they can be fine-tuned killing machines, preying on elk, bison and, in rare instances, humans.

As a photographer, I have watched bears in Alaska's Brooks River Falls, Denali National Park, Yellowstone, and several other places under varying conditions. Throughout all, one conclusion can be drawn: a bear's attitude is primarily dictated by its stomach. When bears have an ample food supply, they are generally content, unless protecting already acquired food from perceived threats, or protecting their young. Predatory bears, however, display erratic behavior, going on the offensive and attacking a passerby or ransacking a campsite.

Camp Run-A-Muck, near Hyder, Alaska, was the wrong place for George Tullos to spend the afternoon napping. If Tullos had known there was a problem bear "stalking" groups of people, he would have found a safer place to sleep and he wouldn't have been eaten by a brown bear.

Each year, Hyder, Alaska, experiences an influx of tourists as 40,000 people rush to see black and brown bears along Fish Creek Wildlife Observation Site, one of Alaska's premier

In the bear community there is an adage—"A fed bear is a dead bear"—meaning a human-fed, or a garbage-conditioned bear will become less fearful of humans and eventually become aggressive or a nuisance in its pursuit of food. These problem bears are then usually destroyed.

viewing spots. During the salmon season the area is filled with bears, running after fish and slapping the water with their paws to dispel the fish into the air, then snatching them with lightening-quick speed in front of wide-eyed tourists. Experienced bears have large bellies full of fish. Younger, novice bears wait and watch from the sidelines, hoping a morsel is left behind. The fish are hard to catch and few scraps are left by the seasoned bears, so the younger ones become hungry and agitated. Some turn to alternate food sources —such as the local landfill, where food is plentiful. At times, Camp Run-A-Muck campers can hear these garbage-conditioned bears rustle past their tents on their way to the landfill. Most bears ignore the snores coming from the brightly-colored domes or the cocoon-shaped forms laying in the open as they pass. But in the summer of 2000, one 400-pound bear became a problem when it started to bully tourists.

Rangers were aware of the problem bear and were trying to catch it. It had already broken into campers' gear and charged groups of tourists if they wandered too close. On one occasion, the brown bear was spotted stalking a group of people unaware of its presence as it used tall grass for camouflage. Traps had been set to catch the bear, but the attempts were unsuccessful.

On Friday, July 4, 2000, George Tullos, 41, from Ketchikan, Alaska, decided a remote corner of the camp would make a great place for an afternoon siesta. His brief stay turned into a nightmare, however. He was attacked by the predacious brown bear. Camp residents later recalled that they heard a human scream coming from a secluded area of camp, but thinking it was someone fooling around, did not investigate.

Tullos' body was found the next day in low-lying brush about 50 to 100 yards away from the landfill. He had been dragged by the bear from the campsite into thicker cover. The bear was nowhere around but its handiwork was clearly evident. Bite marks on Tullos' neck indicated he probably died from the mauling and further investigations revealed the bear fed upon his body.

"He didn't have a tent," Paul Larkin stated in an Associated Press news release interview. "No candy wrappers or food containers were found near his body which could have explained the attack."

The suspect brown bear was found and shot. An autopsy revealed human flesh was in the bear's stomach, confirming it was the bear that attacked and killed Tullos. The bear was not malnourished or underweight, and appeared to be in good condition. No definitive reason can be concluded as to why the aggressive brown bear preyed upon Tullos. However, because of its recent history of following people, digging through tents and gear, and being a garbage-conditioned bear, it can be assumed the bear had lost its natural fear of humans. Tullos apparently posed no threat to the bear, and was an easy target as he had no bear spray or other weapon to defend himself.

SURPRISED HUMANS AND SURPRISED BEARS

In the spring of 1999, I had a surprise encounter with a mini-van-sized brown bear. Totally unprepared to meet the bruin face to face, I can only laugh now because I survived.

It happened in Alaska's Katmai National Park while I was on assignment for *Bears And Other Top Predators* magazine. Carter Mackley, the publisher, and I had traveled deep into the heart of bear country to photograph Katmai's numerous and relatively easy to find bears. Few people enter the park's massive back country, opting to go to Brooks Fall River, the famous place where brown bears gorge themselves on salmon. We were staying at Katmai Wilderness Lodge, an eco-tourism company that specifically caters to bear watchers. Large furry creatures are always close to anywhere you stand — even if you're just relaxing on the cabin's deck.

In the middle of a salmon sandwich, John Bartolino, our guide, calmly said, "The bear is back." My sandwich dropped to the plate and I rushed for my camera gear. In no time I was outside, ready for action.

This particularly pragmatic brown bear was accustomed to people and, according to Mike, the camp cook, it was getting more brazen each day. The night before, it had decided to take a stroll on the cabin deck, knocking over chairs and tipping over empty garbage cans. Smelling food residue on the propane barbecue, it licked and bit the aluminum cooker.

My plan for photographing the bear was simple: stay near the safety of the cabin. If the bear came at me, I would duck quickly inside. But this bear seemed to be a mind reader.

The bear moved stealthily, occasionally lifting its head above the grass to sniff the wind as it moved in my direction. I sat ready for action near the open cabin's door that was just a jump away. Fifty feet from me and moving steadily, the brown bear went behind a large fallen stump and then melted into the grass, disappearing from sight. I looked from behind the camera and saw nothing. I knew bears were masters at hiding, but this was ridiculous — it was just there. I decided to move to the opposite side of the cabin and gingerly look around the corner. Perhaps the bear was heading for the beach to dig for clams. When I reached the corner and peeked, there was no bear. "He must have gone to the beach," I thought, which was only a hundred yards away, down a small hill. With a confident step, I moved forward and came face to face with the 600-pound fur-covered muscle, standing only three feet away.

Surprised? To say the least. It is hard to describe the feeling

When bears and humans meet, the consequences can be deadly for both. The man pictured above found the remains of one of these meetings. The battered and broken rifle suggests the encounter provoked a ferocious battle ending in mutual destruction. (©Knights Taxidermy)

of being close enough to touch a creature that can easily tear you apart. Instantly, an overwhelming urge to run, along with an unhealthy dose of adrenaline rushed over my body. My legs said run but my brain begged me to stay calm. In situations like this, common sense and a knowledge of bear behavior is your best ally.

We both jumped and took a step back. For a brief second, our eyes met and my mind rushed for what to do next.

"Hey, bear!" I simply yelled.

The bear flinched as if hit by the sound. As I took another larger step backward, the surprised bear whirled around, mimicking my undignified retreat. I continued to slowly back up, mouthing some sort of gibberish and fumbling for answers as to what had just happened. As soon as the bear was out of sight, my legs moved so fast the Road-Runner would have been proud.

Fight or flight are a bear's two choices. Lucky for me, my brief encounter ended with the bear deciding to retreat. That is not always their answer. Sometimes, surprised bears fight.

Most bear attacks happen when a human surprises a bear. According to Smith's research, surprise encounters account for 29 percent of all human/bear confrontations.

"A close second, at 25 percent, is curiosity/attraction, which is nearly the same in that the bear is attracted to a person and often a surprise encounter follows," Smith stated.

Surprise attacks are caused by entering a bear's comfort zone, whether intentionally or inadvertently. Depending on the bear and on its attitude, if a person approaches too close and enters its comfort zone, a bear may attack. However, under most circumstances, even when surprised or pushed, bears generally retreat.

PROVOKED ATTACKS

On April 25, 1987, Charles Gibbs and his wife, Glenda, were returning from a hike on Glacier National Park's Ole Creek Trail. At 5 p.m., the couple spotted a sow grizzly with three cubs high up on Elk Mountain. Charles decided to try and photograph the bears, a fatal mistake.

Charles Gibbs was an adept woodsman who loved the outdoors. He was also an aspiring wildlife photographer, having photographed several species, including bears.

As a photographer myself, I understand the adrenaline rush that can cloud your judgment when photographing bears. At the time you think to yourself, "It won't happen to me. I'll just get one more shot and then I'll leave." Of course, that "one more shot" is just after the next photograph.

After discussing with Glenda what he wanted to do, Charles took off in the direction of the bears while Glenda opted to head down the trail to the camper. It wasn't until later the next day

One of Charles Gibbs' last photographs shows the family of bears nervously trying to decide whether to attack or flee. (© Glenda Dean)

that park rangers found Charles' body at the base of a tree, a mile and half off the trail. The last 40 frames of his camera revealed what happened.

The first few pictures show the sow and her cubs, obviously aware of Charles' presence as they moved away from him. As the grizzlies moved off, Charles followed, snapping pictures as he went. Then, not knowing that he meant her family no harm, the mother grizzly turned around and headed toward Charles. The last clear photographs show the grizzlies heading forward into a dip only 50 yards away.

In this case, the grizzly attacked in self-defense. Numerous lacerations revealed that Charles tried to fight off the bear using his arms and legs, but the human body is no match against 400 pounds of bear muscles. Charles survived the attack and was able to walk 145 yards, but finally collapsed, apparently from severe injuries and the loss of blood.

The sow and her family were not destroyed, moved or even

Here, the sow and her cubs are heading into a dip 50 yards from Gibbs.
(© Glenda Dean)

captured. Park policy is to leave bears alone as long as they do not feed on a human body. If they had taken possession of the body, treating it as a food source, officials would have had no choice but to kill the bears. They are believed to still be wandering Glacier's backcountry.

Provoked attacks such as this can be prevented. There is simply no excuse for them. Having said that, I admit that photographers (a group in which I am included), whether professional or amateur, cause the majority of provoked attacks. Call it machoism or pure ignorance, the allure of getting a great close-up of a bear is too much for some to ignore.

A few years back, while driving through Banff National Park, I spotted a black bear feeding along the road's edge. The bear was working over a patch of dandelions and seemed oblivious to my presence as I pulled up to a stop. I tend to be wary of roadside bears. They're accustomed to people and have lost some of their fear of humans. My vehicle caught the attention of another passerby and he immediately pulled in behind my truck. After a loud door slam, the excited family was standing next to me as I photographed the beautiful cinnamon-colored black bear from behind my vehicle. The obviously foreign family consisted of three people: a pushy dad, an unknowing mother, and a scared, wide-eyed little girl about eight years old.

I knew that even when provoked, injured or approached, black bears seldom show aggression, preferring to either ignore people or disappear into the forest landscape.

We stood huddled together, photographing the bear as it rubbed up against the branches of pine trees, apparently enjoying the stiff bristles as they scratched its winter coat. Suddenly, the bear turned to look in our direction, lowered its head, and slapped the ground in front of it. A clear warning sign. I won-

People taking photographs or videos can sometimes provoke an attack.

dered, "Why the change in attitude?" I hadn't moved an inch. When I looked to see what my new companions were doing, I instantly knew why the bear was voicing his warning to us. The dad was pushing his daughter closer to the now clearly-agitated black bear. Point-n-shoot camera in hand, the shaking little girl clung tightly to her dad.

"This isn't a zoo and that ain't Yogi," I thought to myself, motioning for the dad to get back. The dad, ignorant of the bear's warnings, politely smiled at me and pushed his daughter off the road's edge closer to the bear. In the meantime, I could see that Yogi's neck hair was starting to stand up and his head was swaying back and forth. Warning sign number two.

Now only 20 feet away and pushing closer, I yelled, "Get back! Danger!" Just then, the 400-pound bear charged down the hill toward father and daughter. It stopped as fast as it started. The enraged bear huffed, popped its jaw and slapped the ground again with its fore paws. This time, the dad understood the "universal" warning sign and pulled his daughter back. The incensed mother joined the group and proceeded to give her version of a warning sign. I could still hear her as they slammed the doors of the car and drove off.

Provoked attacks are caused by people who fail to heed a bear's warning signs and continue to invade its personal space until the bear feels threatened and finally either charges or attacks. Black bears and grizzly bears react differently to people and require different levels of avoidance. Black bears are generally more forgiving of people's blunders, whereas grizzlies tend to be more easily agitated and provoked. One writer talking about a grizzly's attitude stated, "A sow grizzly bear has no friends other than her cubs, which after two and a half years, even she tires of."

Domestic dogs can also provoke attacks on the dogs' owners. On June 17, 1998, David Mincks, 59, discovered that at times, a dog is not a man's best friend. While checking a fence line on his 80-acre farm, his dog began barking at a large bush. A second later, a black bear charged out of the bush and attacked the dog, giving Mincks time to flee up a tree.

"The bear swatted my dog, the dog ran off, then the bear came up the tree after me," Mincks told the Arkansas Fish and

Game. "I climbed until I ran out of tree, then the bear grabbed my legs and started pulling me down the tree."

Mincks, who did not have any shoes on at the time, kicked the bear in the face with his bare foot. The bear responded by tearing flesh from his foot. Mincks yelled and his dog returned, only to receive a quick swat from the bear. The dog returned again and the bear chased it away, then returned to the tree with Mincks in it, grabbing, biting, and dragging him part way down the tree. Finally, the black bear lost its grip on Mincks and fell out of the tree.

The bear sat at the base of the tree and waited for 20 minutes before finally leaving when it heard its cub bawling nearby. Mincks remained where he was for another hour before finally climbing down out of the tree and running to his truck. Once there, he treated his wounds and drove to a friend's house who took him to the hospital.

Other provoked attacks are inadvertently caused by people studying or trying to relocate bears. Wilf Etherington, a biologist with the Canadian Wildlife Service, and photographer Bill Schmaltz decided to help relocate a garbage-habituated grizzly bear. The 527-pound bruin was drugged with Sernylan and transported to an alpine pass in a remote part of Banff National Park in Canada. Schmaltz intended to film the grizzly recovering from the drug's effect and Etherington, an amateur photographer himself, also wanted pictures.

As the grizzly recovered from the effects, Jim Davies, a helicopter pilot with a lot of experience relocating grizzlies, was concerned about Bill and Wilf's close proximity to the bear. He lifted off the ground, flew near the bear, and hovered over it to assess the situation. The grizzly immediately charged the helicopter, showing little signs of being drugged.

Etherington and Schmaltz continued to photograph the

bear, ignoring its aggressive behavior and approaching to within 140 feet. Still concerned for their safety, Davies landed the helicopter and walked over to the two men. Just as he reached them, the grizzly charged. The men reacted by first walking and then running — Davies first, Schmaltz next, and then Etherington last — to the helicopter. Etherington tried to distract the bear by dropping his pack, hoping it would buy him time to reach the helicopter. It didn't work. The bear caught him from behind, viciously biting at his face.

By this time, Davies and Schmaltz had reached the helicopter and were on their way to help. Upon reaching Etherington, they managed to scare the bear off, chasing it about 450 feet away down a hill. When they came back, Etherington was obviously dead, his face nearly bitten off.

Later, when they returned with park wardens packing rifles, the body had not been moved. Upon circling the area, they found the bear in a brush patch. It charged again, jumping at the helicopter as it circled. The bear was then shot three times and killed.

Regardless if an attack is because the bear was provoked, surprised, or predatory, it is certain that all can be deadly if not met with the proper response, and even then there is no guarantee that a person can escape the deadly power of an upset bear. Learning how to act when traveling in bear country and how to react when meeting a bear in the wild are things that can save your life. Additionally, the more you know about bear behavior and how they will generally react toward you, the better your chances of walking away from a bear encounter unharmed or at least alive.

Weaponless, out of breath, and facing a charging grizzly bear, Chris Widrig turned to meet his attacker. He remembers seeing its fierce, dark eyes as it lunged at his face. There wasn't any time for him to be afraid. The image of the grizzly — open-mouthed, claws reaching out — was the last clear thing Chris saw for over a week.

Returning from a successful Dall sheep hunt, Chris, along with David and Lisa Bjerke, David and Laura Victor, and guide Stacy Keeler were tired and ready to set up camp for the night.

Chris Widrig hiking out after a successful Dall sheep hunt. (© Chris Widrig)

The weather had turned ugly and rainy, and it was time to get off the mountain. They were still high above timber line, heading down toward the Snake River. Base camp was near Goz Lake, Yukon, Canada, and another 50 miles. They were traveling by horse, and it would take at least a day and a half to reach. The terrain was open tundra, rocky with patches of willows scattered about — easy hiking as long as you stayed on the well-traveled trail.

Chris knew the trail well. As an outfitter and hunting guide for 27 years, he had hiked it many times, taking hunters in and out of remote camps. He had seen bears many times, but never had any serious problems with them. August 9, 1999, was different.

"I was walking alone, about 100 yards ahead of the group that was bringing the horses. The trail paralleled a small creek and the wind was blowing in my face. As I rounded a bend, I spotted something partially hidden by some willows about thirty yards off the trail. I realized it was a grizzly with a single cub about two years old. She instantly stood up, ears back, and looked at me. I actually heard her first. She looked ticked and let out a loud 'woof' and popped her jaws."

"I screamed, 'Grizzly! Bear! Bear! Grizzly!' to warn the others."

Chris pivoted to run up a hill, away from the grizzly and toward the hunters with guns, only turning to look back after a few steps. Surprisingly, the sow was still in the same place, now on all fours and just staring, first at Chris and then back at her cub. Chris continued to run. The sow made a move toward her cub, shifted her weight, and charged.

"Grizzlies are amazingly quick," Chris said. "She was running for me fast."

Meanwhile, the clients and their wives helplessly watched

in horror as the attack happened before their eyes. The horses, seeing the same, spooked and scattered with their tails held high, heading in the opposite direction for anywhere else.

"The grizzly snapped her teeth and made a staccato 'haarh, haarh, haarh,' growl as she slapped the ground and charged. Her ears were flat against her head and she was quite vocal. I shifted to fourth gear, but knew in the back of my head, you can't out run a grizzly."

Chris glanced over his shoulder again and saw the bear was almost upon him, ten yards away and still coming. He stopped and turned around to face the bear, hoping to intimidate or bluff the grizzly by yelling and screaming. It had a brief effect. The bear veered to the right, still snapping her teeth and staring at him from only ten yards away.

"It was flee or fight and it was time to fight," Chris said. "I'd done the fleeing and it hadn't worked. I figured this was it."

The grizzly looked into Chris' eyes and suddenly lunged at him with outstretched paws. The last thing he remembers is her teeth and jaws, snapping like scissors, as they plowed into his face. The pain was instant as she clamped down on his head and began to bite and tear at the facial bones around his eyes.

"As the bear crunched into my skull, it was without a doubt the most painful part of the attack, and definitely the most pain I'd ever felt. We were both still standing and she had me in a bear hug, paws around me, and she was chewing on my face. She bit into my hands, sending pain and a sound I can only describe as the crunching of chicken wings. I wasn't moving much at this point."

As the bear fell on top of Chris, now laying on his back, he mentally battled to stay alive. The grizzly stopped chewing on his face and moved its attack to his legs, ripping and tearing at them violently. It bit hard into his fibula and snapped the bone in two pieces. Chris was able to roll onto his stomach.

"Then she started on my back. I was wearing a Gore-Tex rain jacket and she really had a hard time getting through it. Her teeth kept sliding off the fabric. Most of the scars on my back are just indentations and scratches; there were only a few puncture wounds around my kidney area." But the grizzly was able to flip him again.

"She had me on my back with legs spread and I thought it was over, but that's when she hit me with her paws, which was the hardest and most violent part of the attack."

With one swat from a powerful paw, the grizzly cut a three-inch deep, nine-inch gash on his inner right thigh, just missing the femoral artery. Then a gun shot rang out. Dave had fired a shot at the bear, making it run off through the willows, obviously missing it by the way it ran.

Blood was oozing from Chris' face when the other hunters reached him. The light rain, cold weather, and blood loss brought on the first stages of shock. He began to shiver, looked pale, and asked for water.

Luckily, the hunters were trained in rudimentary first aid, but they needed the medical supplies which had disappeared with the horses. They moved Chris to dry ground, wrapped him in dry clothes and started to attend to his injuries the best they could. Some of them huddled around his body, shielding him from the wind to keep him warm, while Stacy and one of the hunter's wives went to find the horses. It took them two hours to find them.

When they returned with the horses, the group immediately went to work setting up tents and gathering the medical supplies. Stacy and one of the hunter's wives, both experienced riders, saddled two horses and took two more to change-off halfway. They would have to ride all night; it was an 18-hour ride to Widrig's base camp. The attack happened about 1 p.m. and by 4 p.m., with the camp's GPS (global positioning satellite) coordinate to give to the helicopter pilot, the two left. They made great time, covering what would normally be an 18-hour ride in under 14 hours, arriving in base camp at 6 a.m. There a satellite phone was used to call for help.

"I didn't sleep at all that night," Chris recalls. "Someone stayed with me, taking turns to talk to me and give me fluids. The bleeding had stopped and I wasn't in a lot of pain. They gave me a Motrin and it seemed to help. I was in pretty good shape, considering."

Opening the tent flap the next morning, however, brought another problem. The weather had worsened. Fog covered the tops of the mountains and the group was concerned that a helicopter would not be able to land safely. The ceiling of mist was low, causing unfavorable flying conditions.

Luckily, at about 9 a.m., the clouds lifted and the distant sound of a helicopter could be heard low down in the valley. Chris heard it first and informed the hunters it was coming.

"It's going the wrong way!" one of the hunters said.

"Well, there are not that many choppers in these mountains," Chris said. "I guarantee you it's ours."

A few seconds later, the helicopter landed just outside the tent with a doctor on board.

At 11:45 a.m., the helicopter flew into Whitehorse and then later to Vancouver. There his injuries were treated.

In less than a minute, the sow grizzly had inflicted severe damage to Chris' body. His nose suffered extensive injury and was sitting to one side of his face, amazingly unmarked. It took over 200 stitches and several metal plates to reconstruct his face

Remembering the attack, Chris says he probably should have done a few things differently, such as avoiding eye contact and not running. When it happened, though, all he wanted to do was make himself look bigger so the grizzly would not attack.

During the attack, however, Chris did the right things when the bear was actually mauling him. He immediately went limp, falling to the ground and trying to protect his vital areas. In a surprise attack, your best defense is no offense. It is important to assess what the bear is doing and react accordingly. If you continue to run or fight, the bear may perceive you as a threat and the intensity of the mauling may become more severe.

It is easy to pick out what Chris did wrong as I sit here in my safe office. After examining the attack, the only thing Chris

Chris Widrig with his family. (© Chris Widrig)

could have done differently is not run. His running may have triggered a predator/prey instinct, causing the grizzly to chase after him. The sow was trying to protect her cub from something she thought was a potential threat. If he hadn't run, the sow may have attacked anyway, but she may have been scared off, too. Keeping your head when faced with a grizzly bear is not an easy thing to do, however. Luck can have as much to do with surviving as proper reactions. Chris Widrig is certainly a lucky man.

BEAR VS. MAN
44

Warning Signs

Photographing bears for a living has advantages and inherit risks. The advantages are obvious: self-employment, working around the globe in wild places, and spending time with a variety of animals are a few. I don't necessarily like danger (although it can be exciting), but I have come to accept the hazardous aspects of the job. When working around dangerous animals, or simply when traveling in their turf, it is essential to know and understand the warning signs given by the animal in order to avoid making potentially harmful mistakes. Being able to "read" an animal's warning signs can keep you from harm.

Early April to Memorial Day weekend is a good time to visit Yellowstone National Park. The crowds are small and the park is full of fresh life as newborn elk calves touch the ground. The young elk are born almost simultaneously, which is nature's way of providing safety in numbers. The large number of newborn elk also floods the landscape with food for predators. In the spring, bears are hungry and the chance of seeing them is high. After waking in early spring, bears spend the first couple of months digging for new plant growth and roots, and searching for carcasses of unlucky animals that have starved to death and appear as winter's snow melts.

On a cold, clear spring morning inside Yellowstone, I was traveling along the shores of Yellowstone Lake heading east toward Cody. I spotted a largish bear in a group of pine trees close to the road with its head down, digging and feeding on new grass shoots. The big animal moved methodically, swinging its head from side to side, searching for the choicest places to eat. Roadsides generally green up first and this road was a blanket of green speckled with splashes of yellow dandelions.

I pulled the truck to a stop and busily loaded film into my camera. The cinnamon-brown colored bruin continued to parallel the road, quartering toward me as I stepped out of the truck and onto his turf. I gently closed the door behind me and inched my way closer, taking a few photos as he walked. As the bear confidently rounded a five-foot sapling and came in full view, I realized he was an old battle-weary male. Through my 500mm lens I could see facial and shoulder scars which recorded years of battles won and lost. He was a large bear with massive front leg muscles and his round belly nearly dragged on the ground. Bigger, more dominant bears have distinct attitudes. They exude confidence and command respect. I did not dare move as he approached to within fifty feet, seemingly ignoring my presence, although I knew he was aware of me. Though nerve-racking at times, when a bear approaches and is aware of your presence, it is better to sit submissively, talk softly to the bear, and let it investigate. This is not easy when the animal approaching you more than doubles your weight and can break the neck of prey twice its size, but it is safer to stay put than it is to move.

Crouched in a kneeling position, I continued to take photographs as the bruiser stepped onto a weathered log lying amongst new saplings. He sniffed the wind trying to identify me. Black bears are usually more tolerant of people and will

Warning Signs

generally ignore humans, only altering their behavior if you enter their comfort zone. If a bear feels hunted, on the other hand, it will run away if it identifies you as a potential threat. The look in this bear's eyes changed the instant my scent entered his nostrils. He lowered his head and violently slapped the log he was on, sending splinters of wood flying. The warning sign was clear; he did not like my presence. I decided it was time to slowly move towards the safety of the vehicle. I heeded his warning by slowly standing up and inching away, taking care not to meet his stare. In bear language, direct eye contact is considered a serious threat. Apparently satisfied with my boorish retreat, the bear continued searching for food and I went in search of other, more agreeable subjects.

UNDERSTANDING BEAR LANGUAGE

Like many large, wild animals, bears are depicted both as cute, cuddly creatures and as fierce, killing machines in movies, stories, and news accounts. It is difficult to learn about their true nature from such exaggerated or simply false accounts of their behavior. Bears are omnivores, eating both plant and meat foods. They are powerful creatures at the top of the food chain, able to defend themselves effectively through their strength and large size. They do not hunt other animals for their primary food source, as wolves and large cats do, but they will take advantage of a hunting opportunity, and will attack violently to protect themselves and their young.

A bear's behavior before an attack offers insights into what it's thinking and can signal the severity and the outcome of the encounter. There are literally hundreds of scenarios, too many to adequately cover, but bears communicate their intentions through body posturing and vocalizations. The more pronounced the posture or sound, the more serious the threat. Bears have poor facial expressions and unlike dogs, do not show their teeth when threatening or growling warnings. It is important to understand their body language in order to avoid physical confrontations. The intensity and duration of an attack can also be affected by your reaction to the warning given by a bear.

STALKING/PREDACIOUS BEARS

How do you tell if a bear is stalking you with the intent of eating? If a bear is staring at you (a direct threat) and moving in your direction, it is trying to decide whether you are prey and a possible food source. It will hide behind any available cover in order to close the distance and to gain an advantage before it will attack. Its head will be lowered and its eyes searching for any weaknesses or places to launch the attack. If the bear

A predatory bear will hide in dense brush and behind trees, stare directly at you, and move closer.

continues to move closer, still staring, even after you make noise and wave your arms, beware. He sees you as prey.

If you feel a bear is stalking you, defend yourself with any available weapon. Hopefully after reading this book, you will at least have bear spray with you or possibly a firearm. But if you have nothing to defend yourself with, pick up a rock and throw it at the bear, or grab a downed log and prepare to strike. Although the final seconds before an attack vary slightly between species, the predatory signs are generally the same. A predatory bear will hold its head low, stare, and silently continue its advance even after you try to retreat.

Tom Walters experienced a chilling encounter when a black bear stalked him. Unlike most encounters, Tom actually video-taped the predatory black bear as it moved through log jams, apparently looking to gain a better position to launch its attack. The video footage is a classic and eerie example of the stalking behavior exhibited when a bear begins to think of a human as potential food.

Walters was hiking when he encountered the mid-sized, 350-pound, dark-colored black bear. The footage shows the bear moving stealthily toward Walters, head held low and eyes locked on its intended prize. Walters tries to move away from the bear but it continues forward, directly following Walters' escape path. Desperation is in Tom's voice as he yells and screams to intimidate the bear, especially when these cries have little to no effect. At times, the bear disappears from view and then materializes from behind a pine tree within arm's reach of Walters. The pursuit lasts over ten minutes until Walters eventually arrives at a lake and takes refuge in its frigid water, while the bear impatiently watches from the shoreline. The black bear finally gives up and wanders into the forest. Walters left the area immediately.

Different species of bears have a few differing methods of

stalking prey. Polar bears hunt by waiting and stalking. They slide across the snow using powerful back legs to propel them forward and closer to prey. Some polar bears, when stalking seals, have even been observed covering their noses with their forepaws, apparently aware of the black color. Black bears stalk prey by moving in a zig zag pattern, gaining ground to get closer to the animal by hiding behind trees and brush. A grizzly/brown bear relies heavily on speed. They sometimes use ambush to surprise prey and can charge the final distance at speeds of 35 miles an hour.

VOCAL WARNINGS

Bears use various vocalizations to communicate aggression, submission, distress and even contentedness, wherein a bear will produce a humming sound. Unlike Hollywood's portrayal of a roaring bear standing upright on two legs before charging in, bears seldom make noises when actually attacking, although victims

Bears consider direct eye contact to be a threat. When a bear approaches, it is wise to evade its stare and to move confidently and slowly away. Never run.

Bears generally stand up to gain a better view, not because they are angry.

describe a huffed breathing as the bear charges. Bears do make complex sounds with specific meanings when they are anxious or aggravated. Polar bears hiss, chuff, and might make a low growl when agitated. The hiss has been described as an almost snake-like sound. Black bears warn people by making a popping sound with their jaw and sometimes producing staccato huffing sounds. The huff might be followed with a quick slap on the ground to warn people they are too close and are invading the bear's space, trying to intimidate those that threaten it by making as much noise as possible. If a tree is nearby, the bear may slap the tree. Grizzly and brown bears also pop their jaws to advertise agitation and might woof or growl when extremely aggravated. The loud pop will generally be followed by a direct stare. Yawning is another expression bears use to show uneasiness and stress. The intensity, frequency, and/or the combination of these vocalizations express a bear's intentions.

Body Warnings

Body language, or posturing, is the most effective way a bear communicates its attitude and warns of its intentions. A bear's body orientation tells other bears to stay away or come closer, illustrates dominance or submission, and portrays passiveness or aggression. Bears use these same warnings and posturing toward humans.

Bears use different positions to demonstrate their size and attitude. In the bear world, being big is important and looking big is used to intimidate other bears, resulting in less confrontations which mean less injuries. Believe it or not, the last thing a bear wants is a fight. A black bear will turn sideways and his shoulder and back hair may stand up giving the illusion he is bigger than he actually is. Brown bears, too, will try to intimidate by size rather than actually fight.

Katmai National Park's Brooks River Falls is one of Alaska's many places to observe bear behavior and to learn the ways bears communicate. Bears there are continually interacting with each other — roaring, jaw popping, and huffing, along with a myriad of other vocalizations and postures.

One summer, I traveled to photograph Katmai's brown bears and the arrival of huge schools of migrating salmon on their way upstream to spawn. The bears were there in full force, and the choice fishing spots were highly prized and, if necessary, violently defended. I saw two heavy-weight champions square up in a brutal fight over one of these spots. They paced back and forth, sizing each other up and searching for any signs of weakness as they roared, open-mouthed and head to head. Their mouths foamed (another sign of stress), and they snapped their

jaws and stared at each other trying to intimidate and avoid a fight. With cat-like reflexes they both struck, hitting each other with incredible blows. They clamped on each others necks trying to get a hold. Their roars could be heard over the boom of the river, sending chills down my spine and electrifying the air. After a few vicious seconds, the loser turned and ran, was chased and then bitten hard on the rear by the winner, leaving a fleshy-looking wound. All of the bears' posturing still led to a fight in this instance, but their battle to establish dominance mainly involved body and vocal warnings. Bears often use these same warnings before attacking humans that are threatening them or invading their space. If you are watching a bear and it starts to display this type of behavior toward you, leave the area immediately. Don't curiously wait to see what will happen, and don't try to get one last photograph. Respect the bear's space and leave.

CHARGING

On October 6, 1999, while bow hunting in southwestern Montana, 40-year-old Eric Burge startled three grizzlies, a sow and two nearly mature cubs. All three bears charged from about 40 yards away the instant they spotted him, closing the distance between them in a few seconds to less than ten yards. Perceiving Eric as a threat to her cubs, the sow headed the charge with her head down, ears back, and huffing as she came. The other two bears, similar in size, followed slightly behind her. Later, Eric, an experienced outdoorsman, said that he had never seen anything move that quickly through the woods. Eric was carrying a magnum can of UDAP pepper spray on his right hip and blasted the air with it as the bear neared. By this time, the bear was only 20 feet away but a cross breeze hampered the spray's full affect. Eric sprayed again with a short burst when the sow was about 10 feet away, causing her to hesitate slightly. He sprayed again. The last burst of the orange mist was discharged at approximately 7 feet and nailed the sow squarely in the face. She stopped cold. The angry bear popped her jowls, sniffed the air, and shook her massive head about, scratching the dirt in front of her as if trying to find a way around the misty field. After a second or two, she decided she had had enough of the fowl smelling spray and bolted over a small rise with the cubs on her heals.

A charging bear is a frightening, surrealistic sight. People who have survived these life-changing encounters describe them as terrifying and dreamlike. Surprisingly, most victims gain a new appreciation for bears after their close-encounter or attack, going on to become vocal advocates for the species.

There are two types of charges: bluff charges and serious charges, and both are knee-shaking, Levi's-wetting experiences. Bluff charges are the most common and are used to intimidate, scare or drive away perceived threats. Most people think that bears stand on two legs to attack humans and then give a fatal bear hug. Bears actually charge in on all four legs and then use sharp claws and teeth to strike, claw, and bite. There are subtle but important differences in a bear's body language that can indicate a serious threat or a "bluffing" bear.

Distance plays an important factor. Generally, the closer you are to the bear before it realizes you are there, the higher the chance that it will actually attack. However, there are no set patterns or distances to accurately confirm this. Some bears might start with a bluff charge and suddenly, without any action on your part, upgrade the charge to a serious one. There are no guarantees.

When in the middle of a bear charge, it is difficult to tell whether the bear is bluffing or not because of your own fear. For example, let's say you are hiking alone and come upon a quarter-ton grizzly feeding in a clearing about 50 yards away. The grizzly, oblivious to your presence, suddenly sniffs the wind and whirls to

A bear's keen sense of smell will let it know that you are human before its eyesight does.

face the odor. Your legs are frozen to the earth and immediately your pulse doubles, sending rushes of adrenaline throughout your body. The bear stares, sizing you up, apparently trying to decide its next move. In order to help with its decision, you wave your arms and talk in a firm yet soft voice to let the bear know you mean it no harm, being especially careful not to return the stare. Its massive head swings back and forth as it sniffs the wind and then suddenly it stands bipedal (standing on two legs) to get a better look. Bears may stand when curious, not because they are angry. Their eyesight is adequate, but their sense of smell is amazing, so standing on two legs allows for a better smell. You force your legs to move and begin the timeless process of slowly backing up. After a quick look around, you find only small saplings that won't provide a safe haven. You know that mature grizzly bears cannot climb trees unless the branches are spaced properly like the rungs of a ladder. Right now, this does little to comfort your fears.

Without warning, the bear charges, running in your direction. Its ears are up and you realize by its body posture that this bear is still undecided. Bears that mean business rush forward like focused freight trains with their ears back and bodies stream-lined. Still unsure however, only after the bear abruptly stops 25 yards away, huffing and popping its jaws, do you realize it is bluffing. When you concentrate on what just happened, you recognize the bear had a loping gait and upright ears that indicate the bear only wanted to scare you away. You, of course, are scared spitless and quicken your backward motion, defying your instinct to turn and run. You know that running could trigger deep-rooted predator instincts and cause the bear to chase after you. Luckily, your hasty retreat is rewarded as the grizzly drops and turns in a fluid motion, and then triumphantly moves in the opposite direction.

As stated previously, most bears only bluff charge. When they charge in order to attack, they take on more threatening postures. The signs are clear and unmistakable. For instance, if the bear's head is low with its ears pinned back and it makes no sound as it rushes at you going full speed, or if it comes straight for you, not changing direction or swerving at the last second, then the bear is going to attack. Victims describe roars and/or growls just before the bear reaches them. The only thing you can do when being attacked is prepare for the hit and cover vital body parts (what to do if attacked is discussed in a later chapter).

It takes tremendous courage to stand your ground when faced with such a threat. A common error people make when a bear charges is to run. This is a HUGE mistake and can trigger its predatory instincts. Standing your ground conveys a co-dominant message to the bear and can buy you valuable time to

decide your next move. Some people believe that bears are unable to run downhill. This is a myth. Bears can easily outrun us — even if we run downhill. I once watched a Yellowstone black bear run down a hillside at a blurring speed as it chased after a newborn elk calf that was only a few weeks old. It was an amazing display of agility and speed.

Other Signs

Prey and smaller animals use effective alert methods when predatory animals are near, and watching for these signs can help you be aware of potential danger too. For example, when a bear walks through an area that is occupied by a squirrel family, the squirrels will chatter incessantly, letting you know they're nervous about something. Once they settle down, you know the thing making them nervous has left the area. Scavengers such as crows and magpies grouped together squawking or just sitting in a tree can mean that there is a carcass nearby. If you are in bear country, it is a good idea to steer clear of the area. Obvious signs that bears leave are tracks, scat, and claw marks

Bear scat is an obvious sign that you have entered a bear's territory.

Stay clear of any animal carcass you find when hiking in bear country. Bears are extremely possessive of their food and will attack to defend it.

on trees. Bears mark trees by raking, clawing, biting and/or rubbing against the trunks, leaving distinct and permanent marks on the tree. If the marks are fresh, be aware that bears may be nearby.

Animal carcasses should be avoided when found in bear country. Bears, especially grizzlies and brown bears, are possessive of these food caches and will defend them fiercely once acquired. If you happen upon a mound of brush, sticks and grasses, sniff the wind for rotting flesh smells and look for deer or elk legs sticking out of the pile. Bears, like cougars, will cover their food for later consumption, sometimes lying on top of the small hill or hiding nearby in a more shady area. If you think it's a bear's prize, it's best to leave the area immediately and not investigate it further. A sleeping bear may be hidden close by and will wake up angry and defensive if it detects your presence. Curious people have been attacked and killed.

Common sense in bear country is your strongest defense. Their seasonal feeding habits and nomadic wanderings make them hard to find, let alone meet on a trail. But if you do happen upon a bear, you can increase the odds of surviving by understanding and heeding a bear's warning signals.

The injured bear that killed and partially ate Michio Hoshino. (© Curtis Hight)

Humans make mistakes. Each year when someone encounters the wrong bear at the wrong time and place, tragic things happen. Michio Hoshino met one of these bears and it took his life. The effects of that day, August 8, 1996, will be forever felt by family, friends, and professional associates who admired his driven quest for outstanding photography.

Michio Hoshino was a man possessed to do whatever it took to get a great image. Alaska's determined mosquitoes, a combative moose, Mt. McKinley's harsh environment — all were just part of a day's work for the award-winning wildlife photographer. With an almost amusing simplicity, he lived life to the fullest, making lasting friendships and bringing contagious laughs to those who knew him.

I met him for the first time when I was visiting Roy and Kim Coral in Anchorage, Alaska. Hoshino stopped by to visit. He was obviously a long-time friend of the Corals' and after friendly hugs and greetings, he sat down comfortably on a sofa opposite me. Our initial introductions were exchanged and the conversation turned to photography. We discussed places we had seen and animals encountered along the way. We talked for hours, laughing and exchanging stories.

Michio mentioned he was having problems with his tripod as he signaled me to take a look. Photographers love to look at camera gear, asking, "Is this a good lens" or "Is this new camera worth the extra money?" as we enviously caress and feel the weight of a piece. My first impression of Hoshino's gear was how extremely worn it was. His cameras were battered and beaten; the camera lenses were scratched and wear marks covered their exteriors. Amazingly, through all their scars, they still captured some of the century's most outstanding animal images.

Hoshino grabbed the tripod head, twisted and shook it, showing how loose it was.

"No good," he said in rough English. "Camera shake."

I tightened three screws around the top of the ball head and handed it back to him, gesturing for him to try it.

"Thank you," he politely said, bowing his head at the same time.

"You're welcome," I said. As I was leaving later in the day, I told him how happy I was to finally meet him and that I admired his work. I told him that maybe I would see him around. With another nod we said our good-byes and I left for Denali National Park, where I spent the next three months photographing bears and occasionally seeing Hoshino along the road.

I can't explain the feelings associated with being close to bears, photographing, observing them and laughing out loud as they wrestle with a sibling or scratch their bellies contentedly. They are truly mesmerizing, comical animals to be appreciated at a distance. However, it is their Dr. Jekyll-and-Mr. Hyde nature that makes us love them when they play and fear them when they kill.

It's here, sitting in my office, that I think back on times when I was camping and I shudder at the thought of what dangerous animal may have sniffed my tent or waited and watched from the forest without me knowing. Had I known, I would probably have slept little, camped less, and kept an eye out for nighttime intruders. Ostriches stick their heads in the sand so they don't see danger coming. Some people sleep in nylon tents. Michio Hoshino slept in a nylon tent.

In 1996, Hoshino was at Grassy Cape Camp, a remote and pristine place located on the southernmost tip of the Kamchatka Peninsula in Alaska. He was there to help a Japanese film crew on a program called "Amazing Animals," and he was one of the film subjects. Several other photographers and biologists were also at Grassy Cape, including Curtis Hight, a commercial photographer from Anchorage, Alaska, who was just starting out in the photography business. Grassy Cape Camp was Hight's home for two weeks in late July and early August of 1996. He had been told that August was the best time to be there, when the Khakeetsin River overflowed with migrating salmon. If there were fish, there were sure to be bears.

From Hight's journal (text has been edited for clarity):

Saturday, July 27. I arrived at the lake shortly after noon and was dropped off at the tundra field. I wasn't expected, and I wasn't sure how receptive the current occupants would be to me crashing their party. I shouldn't have been! A few legs into my haul, a stocky Ukrainian approached. I quickly showed him my permit to be there, but he hadn't come to check my permit, only to help. He introduced himself as Andrei Revenko and volunteered to take a bag.

Arriving in camp, I was invited to sit down at a table and he introduced me to his brother Igor. I had heard good things from other Americans about bear biologist Igor Revenko, but I had never met him. . . . He asked me about my previous experiences with bears and I mentioned my contact with them . . . He was pleased I had some experience, and ventured the thought that I must then know not to run from them.

The next news surprised Hight. The Revenko brothers told him that two days before the group arrived, a bear broke into the cabin and raided it, breaking or biting everything inside. The brown bear had pushed against the outside walls and clawed the plywood, leaving paw prints and visible marks on the cabin. Eventually, it broke a window and crawled through. When the group arrived, they fixed the window with a piece of plywood and moved in. Everyone stayed in the cabin except the photographer, Michio Hoshino, who pitched his yellow and gray nylon tent thirty feet from the cabin's front door.

Hoshino loved to camp outdoors, especially during the summer, which is probably one of the reasons he chose not to stay in the cabin with the rest of the group. We don't know the exact reason, however. Maybe he was just being considerate and did not want to wake the others with his early schedule, especially since the cabin was quite crowded. Perhaps he felt he needed to be close and easily accessible for the film makers. Regardless, he chose not to stay in the cabin, but to sleep in his tent instead.

The day Hight arrived, he nervously pitched his tent next to the cabin, about 12 feet away from Hoshino's. He was apprehensive about camping outside because of the bears, but his fear was waning. Around 10:30 p.m. the first night, Hight watched as Hoshino crawled into his tent and then stuck his head out and said in a soft voice, "You'll wake me if a bear comes?"

"I didn't catch it fully the first time and asked him to repeat his comment," Hight later said.

"You'll wake me if a bear comes near the tent?" Hoshino repeated.

"Okay," Hight told him, and he turned in fifteen minutes later too.

Two and a half hours later, Hight woke to a low-pitched digging sound. He listened intently as the sound grew louder. Suddenly, he realized something was trying to break into the food cache that was stored in a small shed behind the cabin.

"I lay there for a while before dressing," Hight recalls, "wondering the whole time if I was overreacting. . . I was surprised no one else woke up."

Hight unzipped his tent and peered out into the semi-darkness. He saw nothing, but the banging sound was still coming from over by the food cache. Cautiously, he walked around the side of the cabin toward the cache. There was a bear jumping up and down on the metal roof of the food shed, trying to break in.

Hight clapped his hands and yelled, hoping to wake the others and make the bear leave. The bear stopped and defiantly looked at the puny figure standing near the cabin. Hight shouted again. Eventually, the bear left and circled towards and behind Michio's tent.

"There is a bear! About ten feet behind your tent!" Hight yelled to Hoshino, who was still asleep in his tent.

"Where?" Hoshino called back into the darkness, his head now sticking out of the tent.

"Right there!" Hight said, pointing at the bear as it walked. "Should I get Igor?"

"Yes, get Igor," Hoshino replied.

Hight ran to the cabin and beat on the locked door, yelling that there was a bear outside. Seconds later, Revenko emerged from the cabin and ran toward the bear. Hoshino, Hight and Revenko, armed only with a can of bear spray (there were no guns allowed in camp) approached the bear to try and drive it off. The bear simply stared at his assailants.

Finally, Revenko approached to within five yards of the bear and sent a cloudy mist of pepper spray toward the bear. The spray fell short, dropping to the ground just in front of it. Now even more curious, the bear leaned forward and sniffed the ground where the spray landed. It had no apparent effect.

For thirty minutes, the three men tried to chase the large bear away from camp with no success. They noticed a large red gash on its head, perhaps caused by a recent skirmish with another bear. Finally, it turned and left when it appeared his curiosity was satisfied.

After the incident, Hight decided to sleep in a stuffy tower that was a third of a mile down the lakeshore at the mouth of

Paw prints were left by the wounded bear as it tried to enter the cabin where the film crew stayed. (© Curtis Hight)

the Khakeetsin River rather than stay in his tent. It provided a safe haven, plus its high elevation allowed for good bear watching when they fished the river. The tower only had one problem, Igor warned him: a large bear — maybe the one that tried breaking into the food shed — slept beneath it. Hight needed to arrive at the tower early, before nightfall, ahead of the bear who took up its nightly residence at the bottom of it.

The salmon numbers around the camp were low and the crew needed more footage of bears chasing fish for the show. Early on July 29, Hoshino, Igor's little brother, and the Japanese film crew left to find other places to film bears and salmon. Only two bears were seen regularly at Grassy Cape: the large bear with the head wound, and a smaller boar. Shortly after the group left, a helicopter landed with a Russian TV station owner. He intended to spend one night, film the next day, and then leave.

During this time, signs of trouble were already apparent. The

bear with the head wound — the same one that tried to get into the food cache — was becoming more arrogant in its search for food. On July 30, everyone watched in disbelief as it ate from a can of food on the beach, apparently left by the Russian so he could film the bear eating from it. Later that night, the boar tore into the helicopter looking for more food. It ripped the doors off in its search.

On July 31, Hight left for a three-day hiking trip up the valley to search for new spots to photograph. It was a grueling hike and he ran into several bears — some were aggressive and some ignored him as he detoured around them. He returned to camp a day early, exhausted. When he arrived, Hoshino and the film crew had also returned, and the person spending the night at the tower reported a bear had tried to break in all night long, looking up at the occupant, apparently wanting him to throw food down. Hight figured, based on size and its past history,

The wounded bear slept beneath the tower. (© Curtis Hight)

that it was the wounded bear. After not getting any food from the tower occupant, the bear nosed around Hoshino's tent until Igor finally ran it off again with pepper spray.

The next few nights passed uneventfully. The salmon had started to arrive in greater numbers, filling the river, which seemed to keep the bears busy — except one. The bear with the head wound came back into camp again and Igor scared it off with the pepper spray. It was the third time the marauding bear had to be run off, which should have been a warning sign to the entire camp.

At about 5 a.m. on August 8, Hight woke to the sound of a boat motor. Andrei Revenko called out in a distressed voice.

"Someone was killed by a bear in camp."

"Here?" Hight asked.

"Yes, here," Revenko replied.

Michio Hoshino had been killed and could not be found.

Michio Hoshino reads at his campsite the night before he was attacked. (© Curtis Hight)

The bear attacked Hoshino around 4 a.m., dragging him from the tent as he screamed for help. The crew ran from the cabin and into the darkness, their flashlights showing a horrible scene. The bear growled when the lights hit it. The crew yelled and screamed, trying to get the bear to drop Hoshino. A few seconds later, however, the bear looked up, grabbed Hoshino's body in its teeth, and disappeared into the darkness.

An unarmed search party was quickly organized and in the early morning light, they searched the cabin perimeter. They discovered the body had been taken into thick vegetation and no one dared enter it without guns for protection.

At midday, a helicopter arrived with Vladimir Ovsyannokov, a professional hunter and special forces officer. Hight watched from a small rise about 300 yards away as Igor jumped into the helicopter and was instantly airborne, hoping to find the bear and Hoshino. The helicopter hovered over some thick cover and suddenly a bear charged out of the brush heading in Hight's direction. The bear turned when it saw the helicopter, but Vladimir fired before it could escape, hitting the bear several times. The helicopter maneuvered again and more shots were fired. The bear finally fell to the ground.

Hight reached the area just as the helicopter landed and the photographer in him took over as he started to document the scene. He was able to follow along as searchers found Hoshino, and Hight shot his last roll of film on the fallen photographer.

The human-conditioned brown bear that killed Michio Hoshino.
(© Curtis Hight)

"He was in pretty good shape. His hands and legs were chewed up but his face and upper torso were untouched," Hight recalled. "I took the pictures with mixed feelings, knowing that they may be useful in finding out what happened."

Michio's death instantly hit newspaper headlines and people searched for answers to what happened. No one can be certain of what took place or why the bear attacked, but Hight has an opinion about why the food-conditioned bear finally attacked someone.

"When we picked up the tent, I saw a number of things," Hight said, speaking of Michio's tent after the attack. "First, there were claw marks on top and there was a large hole on the side. Second, all of the aluminum poles had snapped. Also, there was no blood within ten feet of the tent, and there was no food or food-related packaging [inside the tent]. It also appeared as if the tent had imploded and there were a lot of little things scattered around the inside of the tent. Finally, his sleeping bag was torn open in the chest area and was lying on top of the tent."

"This leads me to believe that something close to the following happened. I think the bear was in the habit of breaking into human structures and the tent was the only human structure that he hadn't yet tried to break into. He came into camp, as he was in the habit of doing, by chance arrived at the tent and followed his pattern of breaking into things. The bear stood on his legs to push on the tent, or climb on it, just as he did the cabin or the food cache. When he did, he found that it wasn't a rigid structure and it collapsed under his weight. The tent imploded, trapping Michio inside and pinning him down. Michio moved and the bear instinctively reacted to the movement. Michio was no longer a recognizable human form, which the bear respected, but a struggling animal. The bear dug through the fabric and found flesh, then grabbed it with its mouth and extracted Michio. By the time the bear heard the human voices, it was too engrossed in its killing mode and disregarded them."

After researching the attack and hearing different rumors as to why the bear attacked, there are still unanswered questions. According to some reports, Hoshino sprayed the ground around his tent with pepper spray, hoping it would keep the bear away. Did Hoshino have any bear spray? If he did, why didn't he use it when the bear came into camp the first time? Hight doesn't recall Michio having or carrying bear spray. The bear was sprayed on three separate occasions near or around Hoshino's tent. Bear spray sends a wide mist into the air and then settles to the ground. When Revenko sprayed the bear, could some of the spray have settled to the ground around Hoshino's tent? If it did, or if Hoshino sprayed the ground around his tent, the bear may have actually been attracted to the scent. Recent tests on bear pepper spray indicate bears may be attracted to the residue left by the spray. Bear spray is only meant to be used as a deterrent at the time of an encounter. Experts say that if you have sprayed the pepper spray around your camp or gotten it on your clothing, you should move camp and wash and change your clothes before sleeping.

The brown bear that attacked Hoshino had obviously been fed by people before and was losing its natural fear of humans. Michio Hoshino spent twenty years photographing bears and he knew their habits and the dangers associated with photographing them. He knew habituated bears are extremely dangerous. Why Michio decided to stay in his tent rather than in the cabin when there was a rogue bear in the vicinity trying to find food remains a mystery.

Michio did everything right as far as safety and reaction. He

Michio's tent after the attack. (© Curtis Hight)

was an experienced outdoorsman. His camp was kept clean and there was no visible food in his tent for the bear to find. When the bear attacked him on that horrible night, he fought back, and struggled to let it know he was a human and not the bear's normal food. However, a bear that already showed signs of trouble and who was losing its fear of humans should not have been ignored or taken so lightly. This tragedy was preventable.

BEAR VS. MAN
80

How to Survive a
Bear Attack

It's dark when an ominous shadow approaches your thin-walled, two man tent. You know it's a bear; you can hear its labored breathing and inquisitive sniffing. It's close, too close. The bear's claws scratch the rocks as it walks. Each step sends your emotions skyrocketing, immediately shaking your judgment. Suddenly, the tent wall shakes as the animal tugs at its supports. It huffs and then pushes against the nylon wall. You lie paralyzed in your sleeping bag, unable to move.

Do you know how to defend yourself against a bear attack? If a grizzly bear attacks, should you play dead or fight it? What if a black bear attacks — would you know what to do? Should you react differently to a bear that bites and claws your sleeping bag while you are in it? Would you know how to survive?

The answers to these questions vary with each encounter, circumstance, and type of bear involved. For instance, a grizzly will sometimes charge in, swat, bite and then leave. Black bears, on the other hand, may continue the attack. Even the location of the encounter can affect the outcome. Trees can offer shelter from a grizzly but not from a black bear. Fortunately, few people experience firsthand the power a bear can unleash on the human body. Survivors simply describe a feeling of helplessness.

Bears are incredibly strong and lightning quick. Bizarre stories of grizzly bears killing equally-sized African lions with a single blow to the neck have been recorded as amazing testaments of their power. Gary Brown, in his book *Great Bear Almanac*, recounts the story of a man-eating lion pitted against a grizzly bear. According to the account, it was over before the audience knew what had happened. The California grizzly handled the African lion like a house cat would handle a mouse, killing it almost instantly. Another story recounted by Brown was of an American black bear that was attacked by a lion during a circus act. The lion pounced on the back of the bear and a fierce fight ensued. Both animals were injured, but the lion's injuries were so severe that it had to be destroyed while the bear survived.

Trying to measure a bear's strength is difficult. A good but untestable theory is that a 100-pound black bear is 10 times stronger than an equally-weighted man. Grizzlies, of course, are muscled heavier and, in turn, are much stronger than black bears. I once watched a yearling grizzly effortlessly flip over a huge rock that I estimated to weigh between two and three hundred pounds using its young shoulder muscles. It was a remarkable show of strength at such an early age. With all of this power, it seems a miracle that a person can survive a bear attack, but people do live to tell their stories.

The extent of injury inflicted by a bear depends on whether the attack is defensive or offensive. Defensive attacks happen when a bear feels threatened or when it is surprised. The bear will usually rush in, slap the person around, and then leave. Often in a defensive attack, a bear seems to hold back, trying to eliminate the threat, but not kill it. An offensive attack is predatory; the bear intends on feeding. In offensive attacks, the bear

IF YOU SEE A BEAR

AT 100 YARDS:
- DON'T RUN!
- AVERT YOUR EYES — DO NOT STARE AT A BEAR!
- BACK AWAY SLOWLY UNTIL THE BEAR IS OUT OF SITE OR YOU HAVE REACHED A SAFE PLACE.

AT 75-300 FEET:
- DON'T RUN!
- SHOUT LOUDLY IN AN AUTHORITATIVE VOICE.
- WAVE YOUR ARMS AND HOLD YOUR JACKET OPEN TO APPEAR LARGER.
- AVERT YOUR EYES.
- BACK AWAY SLOWLY AND LOOK FOR HIGHER GROUND TO MAKE YOURSELF LOOK BIGGER.
- IF YOU LOSE SIGHT OF THE BEAR, WATCH YOUR BACK AS YOU CONTINUE TO LEAVE THE AREA.

AT 5-25 FEET:
- DON'T RUN!
- HAVE A WEAPON READY — IF YOU DON'T HAVE PEPPER SPRAY OR A FIREARM, THROW A STICK OR ROCK.
- YELL LOUDLY!
- STAND YOUR GROUND AND TRY TO MAKE YOURSELF APPEAR AS LARGE AS POSSIBLE.
- LEAVE YOUR BACKPACK ON.

IF ATTACK IS IMMINENT:
- DROP TO THE GROUND, FACE DOWN, WITH LEGS STRETCHED OUT.
- INTERTWINE YOUR FINGERS BEHIND YOUR NECK WITH YOUR ELBOWS CLOSE TOGETHER
- PROTECT YOUR VITALS (STOMACH, NECK, HEAD) — IF THE BEAR FLIPS YOU OVER, TRY TO KEEP ROLLING UNTIL YOU ARE FACE DOWN AGAIN.
- DEPENDING ON THE TYPE OF BEAR AND ATTACK, YOUR ACTIONS WILL DIFFER.

IF ATTACKED BY A BLACK BEAR
- DO NOT PLAY DEAD — IF A BLACK BEAR DOESN'T STOP AN ATTACK, YOU MUST FIGHT.
- DO NOT CLIMB A TREE!
- DO NOT RUN!

IF ATTACKED BY A BROWN/GRIZZLY BEAR
- PLAY DEAD!
- CLIMB A TREE IF ITS BRANCHES ARE NOT STURDY ENOUGH TO SUPPORT THE GRIZZLY OR SPACED SO IT CAN FOLLOW.
- DO NOT RUN!
- DO NOT PLAY DEAD IF ATTACK OCCURS AT NIGHT!

BLUFF ATTACK
- EARS UP
- VEERS THE DIRECTION OF THE CHARGE, ESPECIALLY AT THE LAST MINUTE
- LOPING GAIT
- POPS JAWS OR HUFFS

REAL ATTACK
- EARS PINNED FLAT AGAINST HEAD
- CHARGES DIRECTLY AT YOU
- RUNS AT FULL SPEED
- MAKES NO SOUND AND STARES DIRECTLY AT YOU

kills the intended prey as quickly as possible in order to avoid injury to itself. It is important to note that a defensive attack can escalate into an offensive attack. The bear might start with intentions of only removing the threat, but then become predatory.

The power and agility exhibited by a bear as it hunts is an impressive sight. Each bear has its own killing technique, taught by its mother or learned through trial and error. One of these attack methods, generally associated with human/bear interactions, is to lunge at prey. When an animal tries to run away from a bear, the bear pursues at speeds up to 35 miles an hour. When the prey is within reach, the bear springs forward, jumping onto the animal's back. Its weight sends both animals crashing to the ground, where the brunt of the attack is on the head and neck area, quickly killing the animal.

Bears attack humans in the same manner, knocking them to the ground and then inflicting the majority of the wounds around the head and neck — it is important to protect these areas. Depending on the attack, kicking legs and swinging arms receive cuts and lacerations — most not life-threatening injuries — so use them as a shield.

Let's say you are hiking alone when you spot a large, humped-backed grizzly 100 yards away, headed in your direction. The wind is in your face and the bear is unaware of your presence. There is no tree to climb. What should you do?

Never run from a bear. Running will only cause an otherwise non-aggressive bear to chase and possibly attack. The only exception to running is when you think you can make it to a tree or the safety of a vehicle before the bear reaches you. If the bear has not acted aggressively and is unaware of your presence, back away slowly and do not stare directly at it. Keep your head down and move it side-to-side, catching glimpses of the bear's attitude and position. Continue to back away, never losing sight of the

This brown bear was scared off by a well-placed (though lucky) hit by a rock.

bear until it is either out of sight or you have reached a safe place.

If the bear is 75 to 300 feet away, shout loudly in an authoritative voice and wave your arms to make it aware of your presence. You want to let it know that you are human. Bears' eyesight is adequate, but not great, so talking or yelling lets the bear identify you. Back away slowly and look for higher ground. Higher positions will make you appear bigger and give you an advantage. Try to look as large as possible and walk confidently. Avoid eye contact as direct stares are considered threatening and may provoke an attack. If the bear disappears from sight, continue to slowly move away and watch your back. Predatory bears often use available cover to get close before they attack.

A rock can deter a curious or undecided bear. On a recent trip to Katmai Wilderness Lodge inside Katmai National Park, I traveled with guide John Bartolino as we searched for brown bears along the coast. John is an experienced outdoorsman and has dealt with several problem bears around the area. He and I were heading to the beach one afternoon when we noticed a sub-adult bear tearing apart the inside of our boat. We yelled and waved our arms, trying to intimidate the bear, but it held its ground, popping its jaw defiantly. Fearing more damage to the boat, John picked up a golf ball-sized rock and fast-pitched it at the bear, later saying he was aiming for the rump. The misdirected strike hit the bear square in the jaw, making a loud crack when it struck. The bear freaked out! He spun, fell out of the boat, and high-tailed it into the tall grass.

If the bear keeps coming and gets to within 5 to 25 feet, have your weapon of choice ready. If you are carrying bear spray, fire the can into the bear's face and reinforce it with more yelling. If you are weaponless, keep talking to the bear and stand your ground. Make yourself appear as large as possible by raising your coat or holding it wide open. If you have a backpack, leave it on as it will help protect your back. If you believe an attack is imminent, prepare for the worst.

Recent advice of bear experts is to lie flat on the ground, face down, legs outstretched. (Some experts advise to curl up in a tight ball instead of stretching out your legs, but all agree to protect your vitals.) Intertwine and lock your fingers behind your neck with elbows close together to help protect your face and neck. If the bear hooks its claws into your side and flips you over, use the momentum of the roll to continue the motion until face down again.

Predacious bears require stronger reactions on your part. If the bear does not let up and continues to attack or begins to lick

Approaching a wild bear is dangerous. Never intentionally approach a bear; it can be deadly for both you and the bear.

A black bear's claws are hooked, making the bears excellent tree climbers (better than you).

your wounds, it intends to eat you. Your only chance for survival is to fight like mad, anyway you can.

If you are in a group and encounter a bear, your best defense is to cluster into one large mass with a solid commitment not to run. The bear will not be able to distinguish individual members of the group unless someone breaks free. Yelling, clapping, and roaring in unison will make you collectively appear large and threatening, making an attack on the group unlikely. Make sure everyone in your group understands this before the hike, as panic often makes people scatter.

Remember that your brain is your best defense, so use it when in bear country. Give the bear the respect it deserves and stay out of its comfort zone if at all possible. Some attacks happen to people who follow all the rules while other people are simply in the wrong place at the wrong time. The following discusses what to do when each species attacks.

BLACK BEARS

Although more tolerant than their cantankerous cousin, the grizzly, black bears can inflict a tremendous amount of damage in a short period of time. They attack by using powerful forearms to hold their victims close, swatting and raking with sharp, hooked claws, while at the same time biting and ripping flesh. Some say a black bear attack is more severe than a grizzly attack because a black bear will continue to maul its victim, whereas a grizzly will often stop if it feels the threat is gone, which is why playing dead works with a grizzly but not with a black bear.

Never climb a tree if you encounter an aggressive black bear. When black bears fight each other, the loser sometimes climbs a tree to seek shelter, thus eliciting a pursuit response from the winner. Hooked claws make them extremely good climbers (better than you), so it is unwise to use a tree when trying to avoid a black bear. Mature grizzlies and brown bears, on the other hand, are not good climbers; their claws are longer and less curved than a black bear's. This is not to say they cannot climb. Small grizzly/brown bear cubs can climb trees. Even adult grizzlies have been known to climb trees by using the limbs like the rung of a ladder, pulling themselves up.

Do not play dead when a black bear attacks. Playing dead can kill you. If you surprise a black bear, it charges and makes contact, you will need to determine whether the bear plans on continuing the attack. If you think it will, you should fight it. Use any weapon you can find to fend off the aggressive bear and go on the offensive, especially if you think it is trying to eat you. Throw rocks, swing a stick, throw dirt in its face, scream, kick, bite, and claw — anything to get it to leave you alone. Perhaps you will get lucky.

Nine-year old Krystal Gadd and her grandfather, George, experienced firsthand the terrifying extremes a food-conditioned black bear will go to when it's hungry.

Shortly after midnight, on the shores off Utah's Strawberry Reservoir, George awoke to the sound of screaming outside his camper trailer. Grabbing a heavy, square-shaped flashlight, he walked barefoot into the darkness and found a huge black bear had broken the window of his truck shell.

"It was a bear, trying to eat my granddaughter," Mr. Gadd said.

As he ran to save Krystal, somehow the bear managed to pull her through the window, sleeping bag and all, and began to drag her down the road as she screamed for help.

"The attack did not need to happen," George said. "They [the Forest Service] were aware of the problem. A volunteer staying at the campground told me he had warned his superiors about a big bear eating out of a parked garbage trailer. Another person encountered a large curious black bear in the area at a phone booth. A passing car finally scared the aggressive bear away. Then, a bear chased Janet Knudsen into her cabin several times."

When George ran at the bear shouting, he expected it to drop Krystal and run away. It didn't. Instead, it picked up its pace, dragging the young girl another 50 yards. Luckily, the bear came to a barbed wire fence, which slowed its progress. The bag tangled in the fence and Mr. Gadd was able to catch up.

"It's kind of hard to watch something try to kill your grand-daughter," he said later in an interview at the hospital.

Jumping the fence, he positioned himself between the bear and Krystal and lifted her over the fence. The bear rose, standing to its full height, trying to intimidate his competition, then dropped to all fours and aggressively came at George. Armed only with the flashlight, he smacked the bear square on the snout causing it to rethink the situation.

By this time, Krystal was out of the bag, standing next to her grandpa as he confronted the much bigger animal. Busy with the bear, he told Krystal to make a run for the trailer.

"He made noise and I made a louder noise. I didn't know what else to do," he said.

As she made her escape, George kept hitting the bear with the flashlight and shining the light in its eyes. Seconds later, he was able to climb the fence himself and head for the trailer. The bear followed closely.

As they reached the truck, George threw Krystal inside and checked the back of the truck where her 12-year-old brother, Jason, was still asleep — he had slept through the entire ordeal. The bear stood about 20 feet away and watched, apparently pondering its next move. Its indecision was short lived.

"I tried to run him down," George said. "He ran over the mountain before I could get him."

As they raced for Heber City, the closest town with a hospital, Jason comforted Krystal. "I didn't think she would make it," Mr. Gadd said. "She looked terrible."

Krystal suffered severe lacerations to her scalp, arms and legs that took doctors five hours to clean and bandage. They recommended a series of vaccinations just in case the bear was rabid.

Shane Cornwall, a hunter with the Department of Agriculture, and Earl Sutherland, of the Division of Wildlife Resources, headed to the area to find the bear. The men used dogs to track it from Soldier Creek campground, where Krystal was mauled, to the shore of the reservoir where it crossed. Later, the dogs encountered and had a brief skirmish with the bear. Cornwall fired a shot at the bear as it fought with his dogs, but after an apparent hit, it broke off the attack and ran deeper into the woods. They never found the bear's body despite numerous efforts.

George reacted correctly to the attacking black bear. He hit it in the snout with what he had available — the flashlight — and he offensively went after the bear. With a black bear, being aggressive and fighting back is the best idea to scare away a curious bear or to fend off an attack.

A sow grizzly with cubs is extremely dangerous—never approach a family group or get between the sow and her cubs.

Grizzly/Brown Bears

The best response to a defensive or surprise attack by a grizzly or a brown bear is to play dead. This is not easy when a 400-pound animal is biting and tearing at your body, but lying still with your eyes closed is your best chance for survival. The bear may scratch, sniff, or bite. You should then pray that it leaves. Do not move or look around until you are sure the bear has left. Listen for the bear's breathing or the sound of it moving away. If the bear doesn't leave, it is imperative not to move. It may be sitting quietly close by, watching for any movement. The slightest motion could invoke another attack and it will continue until it thinks the threat is gone or you are dead.

A grizzly with cubs is North America's most feared and aggressive land mammal. Never approach a family group on foot or get between the sow and her cubs. The younger her cubs, the smaller her comfort zone will be. Sow grizzlies are very protective and if she perceives you as a threat, she will charge and attack.

In October 1986, Tim Christie, a professional photographer, was taking pictures of a whitetail deer in Montana's Glacier National Park when he surprised a sow grizzly with a cub. The whitetail winded the bear about the same time the cub saw Tim. It let out a bawl for its mother and she came quickly to its defense. Tim climbed the nearest tree, followed by the sow grizzly, which used the branches like the rungs of a ladder to get up the tree. She grabbed his foot but, fortunately, it was Tim's lucky day. His tennis shoe slipped off into the bear's mouth, sending her crashing to the ground. Regaining her composure, she stood and let out a woof, then disappeared into the forest.

If a grizzly attack turns predatory — it doesn't stop the attack, it starts licking your wounds, or it tries to carry you off — then you must fight back to survive. Without a firearm or pepper spray, you are virtually defenseless against the power of a grizzly bear. This doesn't mean you shouldn't try. Luck has as much to do with survival as anything else, and the stick you wield may hit an eye or the rock you throw may hit just the right spot on its nose for it to think about you differently.

Polar Bears

The largest carnivore on land is the polar bear. They are extremely successful hunters and are very curious, often exploring human encampments. Of course, as polar bears live in the sub-arctic, not as many people run into them as they do grizzly and black bears.

Polar bears live in a harsh environment. Six out of ten cubs die in their first year. Like other mother bears, polar bear sows raise their cubs for two-and-half years and then chase them off. A sow is then receptive to males again, and she knows large males will try to kill the cubs if they are still with her. On their own for the first time, young cubs will take seven years to fully mature and become master seal hunters like their mothers. Meanwhile, in their developing years, they often go hungry.

Hungry sub-adults are considered by many to be the most dangerous bears on ice. Others argue that seal hunting polar bears in mid-winter can be the most aggressive toward humans. Both are deadly. Any unwary, unarmed human doesn't stand a chance against either bear that decides to stalk them. Polar bears are masters of disguise and are able to blend into the frozen landscape. Patient hunters, polar bears will sit for hours waiting for a seal to expose itself out of its breathing hole, and then kill it with a hook from a powerful paw.

The best advice against a polar bear attack is to be extremely wary of these curious killers and never travel alone. Carry bear spray or a firearm. Be aware of your surroundings and detect the bear before it detects you. If the polar bear attacks, try to defend yourself. Many who live in polar bear country own specially trained dogs that will warn of an approaching polar bear and then antagonize the bear to drive it way.

ATTACKS AT NIGHT

It is extremely dangerous to hike after dark in bear county. Bears are efficient predators at night. Nighttime attacks generally occur while a person is sleeping, either in a tent or out in the open. Bears are curious creatures. A camper's tent pitched near a well-traveled trail or a preferred food source has a high chance

Greg Pierson stands by the food shelter in Katmai National Park's Brooks Falls camp.

of being investigated by a passing bear. Be aware of your surroundings before establishing camp. Look around the site for bear activity or markings. Pick your site wisely and consider possible escape routes such as trees or vehicles. If a bear comes into camp, you need to know what to do.

Do not play dead if a bear attacks at night because the bear is looking for food. If you play dead, the bear may not recognize you as a human. Scream, kick, hit and stab the bear with anything you have. It is extremely important to let the bear know that you are not its normal food source. If you are camping in a group, stay close together and act aggressively toward the bear by yelling and banging pots and pans, which in turn will instill a negative association with humans.

In Katmai's Brooks Falls camp, overnighters are taught to make as much noise as possible when a bear comes close to camp. One day while taking an afternoon nap, I heard a shrill scream not far from my campsite. Seconds later, I heard people hollering and banging pans. I later found out that a Swedish woman woke to find a brown bear's head filling the entrance to her tent. The bear grabbed one of her shoes and disappeared. The shoeless woman, along with the rest of the camp, then chased the young bear away. She never recovered her shoe.

ATTACKS ON HUNTERS: A GROWING PROBLEM

Alaska Fish and Game Department warns hunters on Kodiak Island — home to 3,000 brown bears — to hunt only with a partner. When one person kills an animal, the other is advised to stand guard as the hunter prepares the animal to be packed out. The reason? Some Kodiak brown bears have learned that a gunshot means an easy meal. When Kodiak bears hear a gunshot, they have been known to investigate rather than run from the sound. Leaving carcasses overnight in remote areas and gut piles from the cleaned deer have taught and reinforced this behavior.

Montana Fish, Wildlife and Parks, asks bow hunters to be aware of grizzly bears frequenting the areas they intend to hunt. Archery hunters usually hunt alone, stalking quietly, trying to surprise their game. Their hushed footsteps often bring them dangerously close to bears, when suddenly a bow and arrow are inadequate. Wyoming Game and Fish advises hunters to carry a can of Environmental Protection Agency (EPA)-approved bear pepper spray while hunting.

Most states where grizzly bears live advise these warnings. All advocate not to leave carcasses overnight. If circumstances dictate that you must leave a downed animal, wildlife agencies say they should be left in a large clearing or an area where you can see the carcass from at least 200 yards away in order to avoid surprising a bear that may have found it during the night. If the carcass is partially buried when you return, be especially wary. A bear has probably claimed it for its own. It is wise to let the bear have it. Do not try and take it back.

Animal owners must also be wary of a bear if it attacks livestock (a very rare instance). John Blaine and his wife were sleeping at their home in Butler Creek, Montana, when they were awakened around 12:30 a.m. by a distressed llama call. Grabbing his rifle, Blaine went to investigate the sound. When he found the llama — which was still alive — his flashlight illuminated a black bear feeding on the animal. The bear immediately charged. Blaine was able to kill the bear, but not until it was within two feet from where he stood.

SURVIVING THE ATTACK

Many people who die from bear attacks do so after the bear has left — by bleeding to death. It is just as important to get out of the woods and seek help as it is to survive the actual attack. Blood loss is the primary concern after a mauling. It is important to stay as calm as possible and to walk, not run, out of the woods. Running will make your blood circulate quicker, which in turn will make you lose blood faster and keep the blood from clotting. The most important thing is to try to remain calm so that you keep your wits about you. Basic first aid, the signs of shock, how to tie a tourniquet or make a splint — knowledge of all of these things will help you stay alive if you can stay calm enough to apply them. Panic will only lead to poor decisions and a tragic outcome.

There is no definitive way to survive a bear attack. Each situation requires different responses and some luck. Unfortunately, the bear usually dictates the outcome. The best way to survive an

Bears are masters at hiding and sometimes it is hard to know they are there. Dense vegetation can conceal even the largest of bears. This bear is scratching his back on a tree.

attack is to avoid an encounter. Let bears know you are there by talking loudly or singing. Never hike alone. Avoid areas that bears frequent. Carry bear spray (a *large* can). Be aware of your surroundings. Learn as much as you can about bear behavior if you are going to be hiking, camping, or hunting in bear country, and then stay alert to and respect their presence.

"The grizzly mirrored our direction, 75 yards away, moving through the trees as we hiked down the mountain trail. It was a mother with two cubs, curiously watching us as we walked and contemplated her next move."

Terry Everard and his buddy, Lonnie Schultz, from Laramie, Wyoming, pulled their spike camp and were on their way to the main hunting camp when they encountered a grizzly bear.

"She let out a loud woof and her cubs started to run," Terry said. "She followed them and then stopped about 60 yards away from us, stood up on her hind legs, sniffed in the air and stared at us with beady little eyes. The cubs were still running away. We stopped, loaded our guns, and stood side by side in case she charged. The sow dropped to her feet and disappeared."

As with most bear encounters, Schultz and Terry's meeting ended with the bear heading in the opposite direction. But four days later, a mile and a half from that spot in a dark timber patch, Terry encountered another grizzly, or perhaps it was the same one, but this time, the outcome was much worse.

Terry Everard was an experienced outdoorsman. Having worked for the United States Department of Agriculture, he knew how to read topography maps and compasses. He took several hunting and camping trips each year. He was also familiar with the Sunlight Basin area in western Wyoming. He knew there were grizzlies in the area and had heard reports that a few troubled bears displaced from Yellowstone National Park might be around too. Incidentally, two years earlier, he had watched a documentary on bear attacks, learning how to protect himself against an attack. Little did he know that the knowledge from that show would come in handy and save his life.

A day after seeing the sow with her cubs, Terry loaded a

The "x" penned on this photo shows the location on the mountain where the attack occurred.

North Face backpack with survival gear, an extra set of clothes, and miscellaneous camping equipment. He left his friend, Viktorin, at the main hunting camp and told him where he would be hunting and approximately what time to expect him back. On the third day of his trip, Terry was about two miles from the base camp and hiking through the terrain. It had rained the night before, which for hunters makes for good stalking conditions and allows a close approach to surprise their quarry. However, sow grizzlies with cubs don't like surprises.

"I was walking downhill quietly, like a bow hunter, in a zig zag motion, when I caught a slight movement out of the corner of my left eye. I turned and there she was. I could tell it was a bear when it stood up about twenty or thirty feet away . . . I could see the top half of her body."

Terry Everard demonstrates the position he took when he knew the grizzly was going to attack.

"As soon as she saw me, I saw her black eyes glare at me and then, without warning, she dropped and became a blurred brown object barreling at me," Terry said. "I instinctively went into a defensive mode. I immediately dropped, face down, and placed my rifle underneath my right elbow so I could get to it later if I needed it. As soon as I hit the ground, she was on me."

The grizzly went straight for Terry's head, biting and scraping its teeth across his skull. Luckily, when he hunched up his shoulders, the internal frame of his pack came up above his neck, protecting it from being bitten. A bear bite to the neck usually quickly kills any animal. The only things exposed were his arms from the shoulders down, and his butt and legs, but the bear ignored all of them, preferring to attack his head. Most aggressive bears deliberately attack the head and neck area, and inflict the most damage to the facial areas.

"Immediately she went for my head and started chewing. She wasn't able to get my whole head in her mouth, so when she bit down, her teeth would grade and slide off the skull and basically lacerate my scalp into shreds. I tried to protect my head with my hand and she reacted by sending a tooth through it. Then she grabbed a hold of my shoulders and punctured the upper muscle in my arm."

The long claws ripped into Terry's down coat, sending plumes of feathers into the air. His body couldn't take much more punishment — blood was starting to pour out of his head and onto the ground.

"The thing I remember most is the amount of force she used to throw me to the ground, and her weight. She was just so strong. I'm sure if she had wanted to, she could have grabbed me by the shoulder and shaken me like a rag doll or ripped my arm off. I was just so helpless. There was such a state of shock when it happened. I just wanted the bear to leave me alone . . . leave me alone and I'd get out of there."

The sow finally stopped. Terry reached with both hands to load the rifle that was tucked beneath him. This was his only chance! He had to get a bullet into the chamber and try to stop the bear. Blood was literally dripping from his head, coloring the dirt in front of him. He knew the attack had to stop; he was losing too much blood. The instant Terry moved, the grizzly immediately ripped into his shoulder again, growling and biting. Somehow Terry was still able to make the action and he spun around, lifted the barrel, and fired. *Boom!* At the sound of the shot the bear jumped, ran around in a half circle and disappeared for a moment. Terry rolled over, sat up, and chambered another round, expecting another attack. He looked out of the corner of his eye and could see the bear standing fifteen feet away, covered with blood that was dripping down its brownish coat, turning it

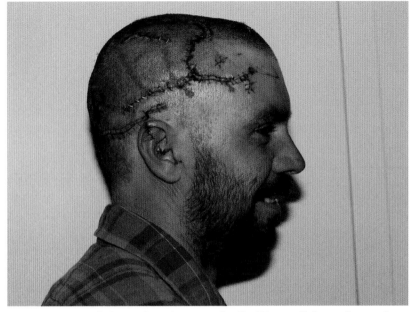

It took over 250 stitches and staples to repair all of Everard's lacerations and puncture wounds, most of them to his head.

red on one side. No matter what happened next, Terry told himself that if the bear charged, he would keep shooting until either the gun was empty, the bear was finished, or he was dead. He wasn't going to go through another attack — not from this bear. She looked at Terry for a brief moment, then turned and ran down the hill from which she came.

Even though the grizzly left, Everard knew he was in trouble. There was a potentially wounded, overly-aggressive bear in the area and he knew its disposition. He also suspected that Viktorin hadn't heard the gun shot from camp, which was still two miles away and around a ridge.

Terry looked at his blood-stained watch. It was 9:40 a.m. He knew that if he wanted to live, he needed to get off the mountain and get medical attention. He dropped his pack and took off running toward camp.

"The will to live is strong. It's amazing what happens to your body when adrenaline takes over. When the survival mode kicks in, you just want to go, go, go and not stop. But I knew if I didn't quit running, I might lose too much blood, lie down and fall asleep, so I slowed to a quick walk and headed downhill toward camp at a gentler pace."

"I didn't know how much blood I had lost or the shape my head was in, so I reached up and touched the back of my head. That's when I felt chunks of skin missing and could feel my skull in different places. My shoulders were really sore."

When Everard came to a clearing, he briefly stopped and fired three shots into the air, hoping his buddy would hear them. His rifle held five cartridges, and suddenly he realized he had only one bullet left. The rest were in his pack and he certainly wasn't going to go back and get them. One shell would have to do.

"The route up the other side was a steep and rocky cliff, so I veered around it to the north and found a gentler place to climb up. Finally, after clawing my way over the ridge, I ran down the other side and reached the creek bottom that was just below camp. That's when I sat down and pondered my next move. If I fired my last shot, I would be defenseless the rest of the way. If I didn't, my buddy might miss me and head toward the clearing where I fired the last shots."

Boom! The sound raced through the mountains echoing off each side. Then it was quiet. He waited, held his breath, and intently listened for a response. Nothing.

"After 30 seconds, to my relief, a distant sound was heard, muffled by the trees."

"Terry! Are you alright?" It was his partner, Viktorin, yelling and heading in Terry's direction.

"A grizzly got me!" Terry hollered back.

When Viktorin reached Terry, he immediately tried to get

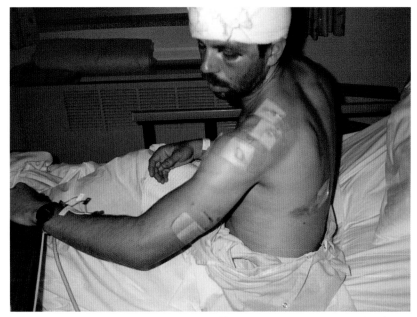

Along with his scalp injuries, Everard suffered deep puncture wounds in his shoulders and arms.

him to lay down, but Terry was more concerned about getting to a hospital. Upon reaching camp, they discussed their options. The decision was made to ride out instead of staying and waiting for help to arrive. Viktorin went to work, readying the horses while Terry lay down. The pain was instant as his head touched the mat. There was a massive chunk of scalp missing on the back of his head and his shoulders throbbed. Viktorin had some pain pills for his own kidney stones and Terry took a couple to help relieve the pain. The pain tapered off a little, allowing him to relax inside the tent as best he could.

After ten minutes, the horses were saddled and ready to go. They headed for the ranger station, about an hour and fifteen minutes away.

"I was sore and there was only one bridal, so I had to ride the pack horse with no saddle. It was a long ride out. We finally reached the truck, watered the horses, and I crawled into the bed of the truck and waited for help to arrive while Viktorin went to use the radio."

The doctor in charge, Dr. Balison, had previous experience with grizzly bear mauling victims. He operated for three and a half hours, cleaning Terry's wounds and using over 250 stitches and staples to repair nearly three feet of lacerations and puncture wounds, most of them to Terry's head. Luckily, he had no broken bones. Dr. Balison did a great job repairing his wounds, which are hardly noticeable today. The scars on his head are now covered with hair. He has four tiny dent marks on his arms and, fortunately, there are no marks on his face. To look at him, you wouldn't know he was ever attacked by a grizzly bear.

In this situation, Terry did the all the right things. He did not run, took a defensive position and went limp, playing dead when the bear hit him. He did not move and protected his vital parts: neck, face and under belly, covering them the instant he realized the attack was imminent. He did not fight back, a wise reaction to an attacking grizzly — they are just too powerful. When he realized the bear was going to continue attacking, he offensively attacked the bear by firing his rifle, causing it to run away. Terry never lost his cool and knew what to do when he encountered the grizzly at a close distance. Then, when the attack was over and he knew he needed to get help immediately, he again stayed calm, slowing down his pace so that he wouldn't lose too much blood, and trying to signal his friend that he needed help. His knowledge of bears and his will to live saved his life.

"The only thing I would do differently — that I didn't know about at the time — is that I would carry bear spray with me because I was in bear country."

BEAR VS. MAN
108

Traveling in Bear Country:
Gizmos, Gadgets, Bells and Pepper Sprays

There is nothing more frightening than surprising a bear in the wild, especially a mother with cubs. When traveling through bear country, whether hiking, camping, or hunting, it is best to try to avoid bears entirely. Even though it may be exciting to see one and tempting to get a little closer for a great snapshot or a look through binoculars, it is best to backtrack and leave the area immediately. The following are ways in which you should travel through bear country and what you should carry with you in case of an attack.

Make Noise

One way not to surprise a bear is to make a lot of noise so that it knows you are coming. Talking, singing and clapping are the cheapest ways to prevent surprising an unsuspecting bear. Commercially-sold bear bells are designed to warn a bear of your presence also. If you don't mind the constant sound of bells while you hike, they work great to alert wildlife. Some people will strap them on to packs, boots and walking sticks, sounding like an invasion of the Salvation Army Santas. Others think it disrupts their outdoor experience and prefer not to use them. Also, outdoor sounds can cover the sound of the bell. If hiking near a stream or even if the wind is blowing hard, the sound will not carry well. It is best to also talk loudly when in these situations. While hiking in Glacier National Park, I have often heard human voices first and then the bells a few seconds later as people approach. The human voice seems to carry better than the bells and is unmistakable to a bear. It will warn them that people are coming and gives the bear an opportunity to move off the trail and out of sight before people arrive.

USE THE WIND

Often overlooked, the wind can warn bears of your presence. Bears have keen noses, able to smell a rotting carcass miles away if the wind carries the scent to their nostrils. Hikers can use this to their advantage. If possible, hike with the wind blowing on your back, which will carry your scent far in front of you. Similarly, if you are hiking into the wind, be aware that your scent is hidden and your chances of surprising a bear are greater. Therefore, make sure you talk or sing loudly, and be even more aware at bends in the trail or near heavy brush patches. If it is a very strong wind in your face, be even louder.

CARRY PEPPER SPRAY

Of all of the bear deterrents, none has had such an impact as pepper spray. When I first heard about bear spray and how it worked, I was skeptical. However, its effectiveness has been proven to work on aggressive and charging black and grizzly bears. It has saved many lives, as the story at the end of this chapter illustrates. Pepper spray has, however, had limited documented success on polar bears, probably due to the fewer number of human/polar bear encounters. Some believe that pepper spray works better on grizzlies than on black bears, but there is no scientific proof to back up this view. Regardless, it is better to have it than not when encountering any type of bear.

Pepper sprays basically use concentrated red pepper extracts, which are measured by testing the capsaicinoids (CRC), or chemical potency of the pepper. The latest, most accurate, and most widely accepted means of gauging true hotness is by testing the amount of CRC in the spray.

Spray should be carried where it is easily accessible. Do not store it in a pack thinking you will have time to unzip it and grab the spray. There is rarely enough time. Instead, store it in a carrying case on your belt, where it can be sprayed from the hip, if necessary. You can devise your own carrying case, or there are now commercially-available holsters you can buy.

Practice spraying the canister so that you know how it feels when it is dispelled and how far the mist carries. Follow the instructions and fire a short second-long blast from the can. Surprisingly, it should have a small "recoil" to it and should spray out in an even mist. My suggestion is to buy the largest, most powerful can you can find and have it with you whenever you're in bear country. If you are ever in a situation where you need to use bear spray, the extra cost and weight will be well worth it. This is not a situation where you want to run out of spray!

It is also important to remember that your aim can be greatly affected by wind, rain, and thick vegetation. The slightest breeze can displace the foggy mist, sending it back into your own face, causing an entirely new problem. The effects of pepper spray on humans include loss of coordination and muscle strength, along with stinging, tearing eyes and difficult breathing. It is hard to play dead or fight after being sprayed with pepper spray.

Canada currently allows United States travelers crossing its borders to carry pepper spray as long as the can states it is to be used only as a bear deterrent. In the past, border patrols would confiscate any spray at the border.

FIREARMS

Guns are not repellents or deterrents. They are used to kill. In some cases, a misplaced gun shot may even cause an attack or increase its severity. People who carry guns tend to have a different attitude in bear country — they are more confident, and sometimes will approach a bear too closely, relying on the gun to get them out of danger.

Bears are tough. They can take several bullets before dying, even from large caliber rifles, and they can inflict severe damage even if they are wounded. Firearms are also often ineffective on charging bears because attacks happen so quickly, often too quickly for a person to shoot accurately. In most cases, even the most skilled hunters are unable to hit a charging animal or to get off more than one shot and kill the bear before it reaches them. Only a perfectly placed shot will kill a bear instantly. If a bear is only wounded, it may be scared off by the hit, or it may increase the intensity of the attack. Obviously, a gun is a better weapon than nothing, but carrying one should not make you feel overly-confident.

THINK BIG

Animals that are potential prey have adapted unique ways to survive. Some lizards fan out a flap of skin, enlarging the appearance of their heads in order to intimidate potential threats. Furred creatures tighten skin and muscles to cause their fur to stand erect, making them appear larger. In the animal world, size

A bear approaches tourists along Brook's Camp beach. It is wise to give bears plenty of room as they go about their business.

matters, and making yourself look larger is a good idea when traveling through bear country.

There has never been a documented bear attack on a group of four or more people, as long as they stood united in one mass against the bear. However, there have been several cases where people have scattered off in different directions and the bear has singled out a person from the group to attack. Bears do not have great eyesight. When they encounter a group of hikers who are standing closely together, they are not able to distinguish each individual human.

In 1996, my wife, Maureen, and I traveled to Halo Bay inside Katmai National Park, Alaska. I was on a magazine assignment to photograph brown bears as they searched the sandy beaches for clams. We traveled with a group of other sight-seers and a guide. A bear approached us all on the beach, and came steadily toward us. Our guide warned us to all stand together in one large unit. By huddling together, we collectively formed a greater animal mass that intimidated the much larger bear, who could have easily overpowered us. We stood tightly holding hands as our guide warned us to stick together. "The bear is just curious and wants to see what we are," he said. The bear came to within 20 feet of the group and then he finally swerved to walk around us.

There is also a new product in development that works on this same principle of size being dominant. Although not available yet, an aluminum frame is strapped onto a person's shoulders or attached to a backpack. The frame holds a self-inflating device that fans out in a partial circle behind the person when it is released, much like a male turkey's tail. The inflated portion of the device makes a person seem three or four times his or her normal size to a bear. It is believed the product will work best on curious or predacious bears, but it will not be able to stop a serious, direct charge.

ELECTRIC FENCING FOR TENTS

High voltage electric fences often used to control livestock have been adapted to deter curious or hungry bears, and other wild animals, from campsites. Battery and solar-powered fences are becoming more popular for campers planning an overnight trip to bear country. They are extremely effective if properly used, sending a shocking message to any bear that touches the fence.

"They were originally designed to keep cattle in but hunting guides and outfitters here in Alberta have adapted them to keep bears away from hunters' camps," stated Joey Olivieri, a Canadian wildlife photographer. "The fences are placed around the tents. When a bear decides to investigate and gets too close, touching the wire, they get an electric shock they don't soon forget. They seem to hate the shock."

The portable electric fences are easy to set up. Stakes are placed around the tent and then a wire is attached to the top of each at the desired height (low enough to walk over but high enough so it hits the animal about chest high). Then the wire is hooked up to a battery sending a charge through the wire. A solar panel is used to recharge the unit during daylight hours.

Karelian Dogs

If you actually live in bear country or travel through their habitat regularly, you could get a Karelian dog. Sometimes referred to as pedigreed pepper spray, Karelian dogs will guard homes, camps and people by chasing bears away. Just like a hound that chases raccoons, these dogs are bred to chase bears. Originally from Finland and western Russia, they will actually run toward a bear, barking, biting and nipping at it to make it leave. They are quite determined in their efforts, using their speed to out-maneuver the larger animal. However, these dogs are only for the serious-minded. Experts advise that Karelians do not necessarily make good house pets. Other dogs are best kept on leash or left at home, as they can actually trigger a bear to attack their owners.

Your Brain

Any of these repellents or deterrents only work if you carry them and use them properly. First and foremost, however, is to use your brain. It is the best defense against a bear attack. A good knowledge of bear behavior, combined with some common sense and a healthy respect for the danger of these animals, can tip the scales in your favor if you happen to be confronted by a bruin.

BEAR ESSENTIALS

- Never hike alone in bear country. Groups of three or more are safer. If the group encounters a bear and it shows aggressive behavior, stay close together and do not run.

- Be aware of your surroundings and keep your wits. Your brain is your best weapon.

- Always talk while hiking and avoid walking near streams or rivers where your voices could be covered by the sound of rushing water.

- Always carry bear pepper spray, preferably the largest can offered by the manufacturer. Carry it on your hip or a place where you can reach it quickly if needed.

- Be wary when approaching "blind" corners or bends in a trail, dark timber patches or thick brush. Bears look for shady, cool places to take afternoon naps.

- Hike with a pack on and keep it on your back if a bear approaches. Do not take it off. A discarded pack may get the bear's attention for a moment, but the pack will provide some protection against raking claws and teeth.

- Carry a first-aid kit and overnight supplies.

- If a bear approaches and you are alone, make yourself appear bigger by opening your coat, waving your arms, or holding your pack above your head.

- If you are camping overnight, hang your food high in a tree at least 100 yards away from where you will sleep. Support the food with a rope between two trees and place it in the middle where a bear cannot climb the tree and reach it.

- Keep your bear spray close at hand while sleeping. If a bear approaches your tent, talk loudly and have the spray ready.

- Do not sleep in the same clothes you cook your dinner in; change your clothes after cooking!

- Watch for signs of a bear before making camp. Look for rubbed or scratched trees, bear scat, and over-turned dead trees where the bear dug for roots or insect larvae.

"She was biting my head," Mark Matheny vividly recalls. "I could smell her rotten breath as she opened her mouth and started to tear at my face."

On a cold, crisp, late-September morning during the 1992 archery season, Mark Matheny and Fred Bahnson, both of Bozeman, Montana, had taken a mule deer. A skiff of fresh snow covered the ground, crunching as they walked back to their Jeep parked at the bottom of the trail. Mark, a well-built, stocky construction worker, and Fred, a practicing plastic surgeon, were both familiar with the trail, having traveled it many times. Their plan was to hunt elk on the five-mile trip back to the vehicle and then return the next day to haul the deer out with horses. It was a well-traveled mountain trail in the Taylor Fork drainage, an area harboring an abundant population of elk, deer, black bear, and even a few grizzlies. By noon, both men felt lucky to be alive. They learned firsthand that there is no good time to surprise a protective grizzly with cubs.

It was almost noon and the men were moving quickly and quietly, scanning the treeline for any movement as they hiked. Mark later explained, "We were hoping to surprise an unwary elk around one of the many bends in the winding trail."

The conditions for their ambush were perfect if only the elk would cooperate. The wind direction was right, blowing directly into their faces, and the fresh snow made a swift, silent descent possible. Mark and Fred were both experienced bowhunters and had learned to step softly so the game wouldn't detect their approach. For the first four miles, they saw no sign of elk or any other wildlife.

They had successfully orchestrated such ambushes several times over the previous 18 years, but it began to look like this would not be a repeat. They only had a mile left as they moved through a thick pocket of trees and walked down a bush-covered knoll. Mark was in the lead, a few yards ahead of Fred, and remembers thinking that it was quiet — very quiet.

As Mark rounded a sharp corner in the trail, two ravens suddenly flew from a tree announcing their alarm with a startlingly loud cry. From the corner of his eye, Mark caught a swift movement off to his left. He turned his head to see what humans most fear when hiking in bear country — a grizzly sow with cubs only 35 yards away. Mark turned in time to see the sow spring to her feet, throwing her three nursing cubs into the air. The large female stared directly at him. Mark had stumbled onto the worst possible bear-human scenario — a surprised female grizzly with cubs. The sow signaled her cubs to find safety with a series of loud grunts and then she charged, with her snout low to the ground and ears back. There was no time to look for, let alone climb a tree, or even draw his bow. There was barely time to yell at Fred, "It's a bear! Get your spray!"

The bear's charge was a blur. Strangely, for a fraction of a second, Mark remembers thinking how beautiful and powerful the animal was as it moved toward him. But then the sow was on him with her crushing jaws and sharp claws.

Fred looked up, surprised to see not one, but four bears, with the big one almost on top of Mark. Fred had two things going for him. The first was courage. The second, a small four-ounce can of pepper spray.

Mark tried to backpedal toward Fred, who was just a few feet away. Anything to buy time, but it was useless — the bear was too close and too quick. Just before the sow hit, Mark shoved his bow toward her, braced himself for the impact, and bellowed, "Get out of here!"

The grizzly swatted the bow out of his hands and slammed

him into the ground, biting anything that moved. As her mouth approached his face, Mark remembers seeing only her dulled, yellowish teeth. Lying on his back, he tried to fend off the fury, but she was too fast and definitely too strong. She immediately pushed her neck forward bringing her teeth and jaws closer to Mark's neck. He tried to stop by grabbing her fur, but it was useless to try and fight. Her jaw wrapped around his throat and tore the tissue away. She ripped his jaw muscle, penetrating a salivary gland and only missed his jugular vein by an eighth of an inch.

Unknown to Mark and Fred, the grizzlies had been feeding. Not only was she protecting her cubs, she was defending a half-eaten elk carcass. Double trouble! She took a second bite, engulfing most of Mark's head. He felt the teeth crunching and penetrating his skull.

Mark recalls, "I screamed, 'She's got my head! She's killing me!' I knew I was a dead man. She was crushing my skull."

Meanwhile, Fred tore his tiny bottle of pepper spray from his homemade leather holster. Filled with adrenaline and unwilling to watch his friend be mauled to death, he rushed toward the sow, shouting to distract her. His prompt, brave action clearly saved Mark's life. A split-second later, Mark's head would have been crushed. The bear released Mark and turned to face the second puny human. Fred fired a thin fog of pepper spray at her, aiming for her nose, mouth, and eyes.

The pepper spray — made of oleoresin capsicum, the hottest part of cayenne pepper — did its job. But then Fred was in trouble. His aim was true; he had hit the sow directly in the face. She reacted with a moan. Not understanding the source of her new discomfort, she lunged, knocking the myopic Fred to the ground. The force of the blow sent both the small spray bottle and his glasses flying. The grizzly, associating Fred with the terrible burning sensation in her eyes, nose, and mouth, returned to

Mark. Ignoring his bloody head, she began tearing at his arm, shaking him violently. Fred scrambled to find the spray.

Mark was pinned to the ground, trying to shield his head from the relentless onslaught of claws and teeth. He realized his only chance was to play dead — easier said than done when being attacked by a grizzly. He tried to go limp. His only thought was, "I am going to be eaten alive." Finally, Fred found the spray lying on the ground. He again rushed the bear. He knew the spray was about gone, and if they had any chance of survival, the last shot had to be close and directly in the bear's face. He charged in close and fired the spray. He hit the sow with a direct blast in her face and held the button until the bottle was empty. The sow retaliated by turning and attacking Fred, hitting him again and knocking him off his feet. This time, she tore into his left side. He tried to fight but knew they were now defenseless. Both men were badly injured. They were out of ideas, energy and, most importantly, repellent spray. Four ounces is not much pepper spray, but luckily, in this case, it was enough. The sow suddenly dropped her attack on Fred and ran off with her cubs, apparently searching for safer breathing air.

Confused, Mark asked, "Why didn't you spray the bear?"

"I did spray her," Fred said. "I emptied the entire can!"

The two men estimate the attack took less than a minute, start to finish, but in that small amount of time she had inflicted severe injuries to both of them. Had she persisted, she could have easily killed one or both of them.

An assessment revealed Fred's injuries amounted to chest and back lacerations, with possible rib injuries. Mark's head had received the brunt of the attack. Blood streaked his face, pouring out of several cuts. One of the bear's canine teeth had actually penetrated his skull above his left temple. A slice of bone off the top of his head was missing. Additionally, the cayenne pepper spray still lingered in the air, making it difficult to breathe.

With the bear gone, Mark stumbled to his feet and Fred (a doctor) began to dress the wounds as best he could. They had to get out of there, not only because of his wounds, but to escape the possibility of a second attack. Fred knew that in their condition and without any more bear spray, they wouldn't survive another attack.

The men were a mile from their truck and there was no way out but to walk. As they walked, they sang hymns and talked loudly to avoid surprising another bear. When they arrived at the truck, Fred took some dramatic photos of the bear's handy work on Mark's head. The injuries were severe but Mark would live. Fred called the hospital to alert the emergency room of the accident and told them they were on their way.

At the hospital, Fred, though badly cut and suffering from two separated ribs himself, insisted on working on Mark's injuries before letting someone attend to his own. Mark had lost a lot of blood and it took over two hundred stitches just to close his head wounds. The dried blood, dirt, and deep lacerations took over six hours to completely clean, stitch, and dress. Then, after Mark was repaired, Fred finally let someone bandage his wounds. The entire time, the smell of the sow grizzly and a retching odor of decayed elk flesh permeated the emergency room.

Nine days later, toting his video camera, Mark returned with a number of friends to the Taylor Fork drainage, the place of the attack. There they discovered a heap of hair and scattered bones — the only remains of the elk carcass. They filmed the scene and he relived the attack. He didn't want to be left with an irrational fear of bears just because he had been severely mauled. He wanted to accept the experience and be comfortable hiking the mountains that he so dearly loved.

TRAVELING IN BEAR COUNTRY

"I can go out there with a lot of peace on my mind," he says. Today, the only thing he does differently is that he never hikes in bear country without a large can of pepper spray. He says of his feelings toward the great bear, "I can't put it in words, but now I'm drawn to help preserve this animal."

Both men told their story to the Fish and Wildlife Service and agreed that the bear was only behaving naturally — it was protecting her cubs and food supply. Neither Mark or Fred feel animosity toward the sow nor did they feel it was necessary to pursue and kill the bear.

As a direct result of his attack and being saved by pepper spray, Mark's life was changed. He opened a business called UDAP (Universal Defense Alternative Products), which manufactures a pepper spray called Pepper Power for defense against animal and human attacks. He also designs and markets Pepper Power holsters, easily accessible belt and chest harnesses, which allow the wearer to fire the pepper spray directly from the holsters.

"Quick access is the key to using bear deterrent . . . If you surprise a bear, your actions have to be instinctive," Mark advises, "so you should wear the bear spray in the same place all the time."

He also recommends that a half-second burst be fired occasionally so the user becomes familiar with the range and "shotgun" fog that the bear spray emits.

"Make sure that when you test the can, to spray it downwind and outside," Marks warns, "and keep it out of reach of children."

Mark Matheny gives the best testimonial for his products because he knows firsthand just how fast and violent a surprised bear can react, and how frail the human body is in comparison.

BEAR VS. MAN
126

Attacks: Are They Increasing?

The following bear attacks all happened in one month, although they are not all the attacks that occurred.

September 1, 2000

Richard Romano, of Belgrade, Montana, was attacked while he sat down to eat a sandwich in Yellowstone National Park. The following is an excerpt from his testimonial about his attack and the effectiveness of bear spray.

"It was a cold and rainy late summer day. I rode for about two hours, stopping every once in a while to glass the area for game. I decided to stop for lunch, and as I was riding down to a spot near the creek, I looked over the area really well. I hobbled my horse and sat down against a tree. I was halfway through my sandwich when my horse started snorting. Since I raised this horse, I knew his mannerisms and recognized that something was wrong. I caught a glimpse of movement on my left and when I turned my head, staring at me from four feet away was a big grizzly bear. I knew I wasn't going to sit there and die. I started to get up, but the heel of my shoe snagged on my rain pants and I fell forward towards the bear. What happened next was fast and furious. The grizzly bear grabbed my shirt with his teeth and ripped it apart. As I began to stand up the bear hit me with his paw right in the chest, slamming me face first into a tree, cutting my face and breaking my glasses. Lying there on my back, I grabbed my UDAP bear spray. By this time, the bear was standing over me with his mouth wide open ready to take a bite out of me. I shoved the can in his mouth and pushed the trigger, sending a blast of hot spray down the bear's throat. The bear went straight up into the air and fell over backwards coughing and choking."

Park rangers later found Richard's untouched sandwich where he dropped it. Deep claw marks indicated the bear left in a hurry, probably looking for a creek to wash its mouth out.

SEPTEMBER 5, 2000

A seventy year veteran of the woods, Max Tylee was scalped by a rampaging grizzly bear while he hunted for moose near Vancouver, Canada.

Max left his wife, Josie, in the truck as he walked off into the bush. Seconds later, Josie heard her husband screaming for help. Calling out his name, she grabbed a rifle and ran to his aid. She didn't get far.

A few steps into the bush, a grizzly charged the 63-year-old lady who ran back to the safety of the truck. All she could do was drive away to get help. When she returned ninety minutes later, Max was lying on the road, still alive but bleeding profusely. The bear was gone.

SEPTEMBER 14, 2000

A father and son were attacked by an unprovoked black bear as they archery hunted in Colorado.

ATTACKS: ARE THEY INCREASING?

"The bear came out of the bushes and attacked the younger man, biting him on one buttock," Division of Wildlife Officer Todd Malmsbury told the Denver *Rocky Mountain News*. "His father was carrying a .44-caliber handgun, but apparently became so unnerved by the attack he ended up throwing the weapon at the bear." The man's attempt to get the bear off of his son succeeded but the bear turned the attack on him, biting him on the thigh. They escaped when a third man grabbed the gun and fired a few shots at the bear. It is unknown if it was hit.

Wildlife officials later tracked the bear with dogs to kill it.

WHAT'S GOING ON?

For bears, autumn is a time of *hyperphagia,* or feasting. It is the final binge before entering their dens to sleep away the long winter months. This time is critical for bears. They need to take in enough calories to endure nature's mandatory fast. They become eating machines, altering their behavior sometimes for the worse. Driven by the enticing scents of human refuse, they venture closer to towns and cities looking for easy meals. Unknown to them, these meals come with a high price. Humans invoke swift judgment, condemning garbage bears as no longer "wild," but simply as pests that keep attacking their garbage cans.

Attacks on humans increase in the fall when bears become hyperphagic. The reason: fall is also the time of year people enjoy nature's bounty. Hunters take to the fields to match wits with their prey and, unfortunately, sometimes become prey themselves. Hikers want to get just one more trek in before they become confined to the indoors. The number of bear attacks directly coincides with the number of people who venture into the woods. The higher the number, the more people run into bears.

Hyperphagia also has an effect on the outcome of bear/human encounters. When bears are hungry, they become

Top: Black bear prints in mud. Above: Bones outside a bear den in Yellowstone National Park, remnants of carcasses dragged home for leisurely consumption.

irritable and anxious, which may cause them to attack rather than flee. Environmental problems can also cause bear behavior to change from year to year. Drought years will often make bears more edgy as berries and other vegetation are not as plentiful. During these years, complaints about problem bears naturally increase. Being aware that a bear may be more desperate for food during a drought year can help a hiker or hunter react accordingly when seeing a bear.

Are the lower forty-eight states experiencing bear population problems or are more people moving into bear country, thus elevating encounters between bears and humans? The answer is both. Studies show since 1993, bear population numbers have increased 75 percent to roughly 700,000 animals nationwide. With this increased population comes an increase in public complaints.

Dogs are being attacked in some states. The hungry bears go after their food and in the scuffle, the dogs get hurt or killed.

Campers in California are experiencing problems with hungry and ingenious black bears. In Yosemite National Park, some bears have learned to hook their claws in between a car door and its frame, and then bend the door down to gain entry. Once inside, they tear through the back seat and crawl into the trunk where food is thought to be stored safely. The bears have even learned which cars are the easiest to get into, preferring Hondas and Toyota sedans. At the time of this writing, 186 bear incidents have caused $634,595 worth of damage to human property in Yosemite. Such behavior brings harsh judgment from humans. Eventually problem bears will be dealt with by removal from the area or death.

A traditional method of dealing with problem bears is to shoot the bear with rubber bullets. This tactic has had limited success, but is still used by many national parks. If the bear con-

ATTACKS: ARE THEY INCREASING?

BEAR VS. MAN
134

tinues to cause problems, the last resort is to tranquilize, tag and then transport the guilty bear to remote wilderness areas. Most of the bears return a few days later. Of these bears, more than half get into trouble again and eventually have to be destroyed.

Mammoth Lakes, California, is experienced in dealing with problem black bears. Steve Searles is a wildlife consultant for the police department and it is his job to reintroduce the bears' natural fear of humans and to teach the 30 or so bears that frequently visit the small ski resort town that they are not welcome.

"It is easier to change the bears than it is to change the people," Searles says in a newspaper interview.

Some Mammoth Lakes residents intentionally leave 50-pound dog food bags on their front porches to attract the bears. This unnatural food source causes obesity, with some bears weighing over 600 pounds. It can also cause aggressive behavior.

On call 24 hours a day and armed only with pepper spray, rubber bullets, exploding flares, and a newly-acquired Karelian dog named Tucker, Searles ventures out to scare bears away from buildings and from the numerous trash bins around town. With so many bears wandering around, Searles is a busy man, responding to 140 calls his first year.

Late nights and charging bears are common for his newly-formed company, called Bear Affairs. Their goal is to use aggressive, alternative, non-lethal methods to deter bears in order to live in harmony with them. When Steve approaches an unwelcome black bear, he approaches as would a dominant, more aggressive bear, assuming the "alpha" bear role of the area, thus speaking a language they can understand. News of his pioneering techniques has reached other regions. He is currently working with Whistler, a Canadian town experiencing the same bear problems as Mammoth Lakes.

Human encroachment into prime bear country is also part of

the problem and it is growing. Bears live in beautiful places and humans want to live in these places too. New Jersey, the nation's most densely populated state, is experiencing severe bear problems. Forests are shrinking and bear populations are growing. A burgeoning community of about 1,200 bears lives and roams around northwestern New Jersey alone. Although rarely aggressive, the animals are foraging closer to town sites, attacking garbage cans left full of food scraps, frightening people on camping trips, and ripping window screens off of cabins to get inside.

"People are fed up," New Jersey state wildlife biologist Bob Eriksen told *Time Magazine*. "All I do is bear control." *The New York Times* reported that the number of complaints had increased to 1,659 in 1999 from 285 in 1995. Among the reported problems were 29 bears entering homes, up from 3 in 1995, and 28 bears around campgrounds and parks looking for food, up from 5 in 1995. Attacks on livestock and pets also swelled greatly since 1995. As of yet, no attacks on people have been reported.

Forged by thousands of complaints, a controversial new hunting season was planned for New Jersey's black bears. For the first time in 30 years, 175 permits were given to sportsmen for the two-day hunt. However, the hunt was canceled ten days before it was to open after then-Governor Christine Todd Whitman asked the state's Fish and Game Council to cancel it because of anti-hunting complaints.

New Jersey and California are not the only states experiencing problems. Wyoming's elk hunters have returned to find carcasses left the previous night claimed by possessive grizzly bears. The bears sometimes retaliate by mauling the usually unarmed hunter. The state's fish and game department has been trying to come up with an amicable agreement for both parties. As of yet, the only thing working seems to be educating hunters about how to care for their trophies and warning them to stay armed when in grizzly country, especially west of Cody, Wyoming.

Colorado is experiencing Goldilocks in reverse. Steve Solomon woke one night to find a 400-pound black bear rummaging through his garbage, peacefully eating a cantaloupe. The encounter ended friendly but because of nature's food shortages, they are happening far too often. A dry summer left the 2000 berry crop in shambles. The bears did not fare much better; 25 were killed in 2000 alone under Colorado's two-strikes-and-you're-out policy. Biologists and state officials say that if there are more summers like that one, and if new home construction along Colorado's scenic mountainous areas continues at its feverish pace, more potentially dangerous confrontations will occur.

In 1999, in a small, one-street town in British Columbia, Canada, called Oweekeno, 200 residents stayed indoors through most of November. The dramatic drop in salmon numbers in streams caused hungry bears to enter town looking for food. Because of the food shortage, the grizzly bears who normally avoid humans broke into cabins, frightening residents.

"Everybody has to be picked up in cars, kids can't come out of school," Tom Gottselig, fisheries administrator for the Oweekeno First Nation told *CBS News*. Nine bears were eventually shot and three were airlifted out of town to remote wilderness areas.

Recently, in Worcester, Massachusetts, after being chased by police through town, a black bear attacked a chained dog. The dog barked and the agitated bear turned on the canine. The bear was promptly shot and killed. Several other bears had also been sighted in and around town.

Edward F. Johnson, with the Worcester police stated, "I've been on [the job] for 20 years and this is the first year we're getting this many sightings, calls and complaints on bears."

Attacks on humans are definitely increasing. Each year more

and more people experience firsthand the power a bear can unleash on a defenseless human body. Increased tourism, housing pressure, anti-hunting influences, along with poor growing seasons, have combined to make potentially volatile situations.

Nancy Mark Honig, an archivist for the internet-based *Animal Attack Files*, stated, "Reports of bear-human contacts definitely seem to be up. This summer brought news of numerous fatalities and near-fatal encounters. Why? Either the bears are increasingly venturing into human territory or humans are increasingly invading bear territory. This year, both of these things are happening at once. Humans seem to be moving their recreational activities and their home-building activities well into the wilderness that bears once had all to themselves. Hikers, bikers and hunters are moving further into remote areas. Prosperity has increased the demand for real estate and people now live in bear country.

"At the same time, food shortages seem to have brought the bears into human territory, resulting in very unhappy outcomes this year in Canada, Tennessee, Alaska and elsewhere."

Mark Matheny, founder of Universal Defense Alternative Products (UDAP), has been keeping records of bear attacks since his deadly encounter in 1992 when he was mauled by a grizzly. He is now an outspoken advocate for the grizzly bear.

"I don't believe attacks are increasing; I think more people are running into more bears," Mark said. "Eco-tourism is booming, sending more hikers into the backcountry where grizzly bears live. As the encounters increase, logically we will have more attacks. We would probably hear about more attacks if it wasn't for more hikers carrying bear spray. Bear spray can dispel the bear and will hopefully lessen the severity of the attack. Unfortunately, the more severe the attack the bigger the headlines."

It is unfortunate that more attacks mean bigger headlines

because publicity can have dramatic and long-term negative effects on both people and bears. News of dramatic, violent bear encounters send biased views to the public, creating undue fear about the viciousness of bears. People fear what they don't understand and can't control. Just as the movie *Jaws* negatively affected the shark's reputation over twenty years ago, exaggerated publicity about the ferociousness of bears will result in a prejudice against bears, casting them as ruthless killers.

Prejudice can kill bears. In 1996, a group of campers stoned to death a two-year-old cub at a Yosemite National Park campground. The teenagers told investigating officers that they were trying to save their food which was found later to be improperly stored. The 100-pound cub died from "blunt trauma" caused by several hits from large rocks. Officers found no evidence that the campers were in any danger and could not find any reason for what they did. The teenagers' chaperones were ticketed.

The opposite response to wild bears is to treat them as if they are harmless or almost tame. Can a bear be taught to come to a feeding station just like a whitetail deer can? Yes, quite easily. But bears will react aggressively if the feeding stops when you go on vacation or lock up the summer cabin. Like a raccoon, a bear that becomes accustomed to finding easy meals on your doorstep will cause damage when food isn't there. All too often, something like the following happens:

The "friendly" black bear mother with two cute, adorable cubs, the one that has been hand-fed off the front porch for the past two weeks, doesn't understand when food scraps aren't there. When she comes in the middle of the night for more food and finds a dark, empty-looking structure, she decides to help herself and climbs through the kitchen window along with her two fur balls. The commotion wakes a frightened homeowner who picks up a gun to shoot whatever it is that is in his house.

The family of content bears is busy searching for food. A shot wakes up the neighbors and the whole community lights up. Suddenly the scantily-clothed homeowner is recounting a tale of horror to wide-eyed neighbors of his near-death experience. The homeowner now has a tale to tell for the rest of his life, and a mother bear is dead because of his ignorance.

Meanwhile, within earshot of the busy house, two newly-orphaned cubs cling tightly to a tree. Suddenly the world seems much larger and more terrifying to them. Their fate is unknown, but the odds are against them. With only a year of tutelage, they haven't learned where natural foods are found. They don't understand why their mother lies motionless in the kitchen. They only know homes have tasty treats and are easy to break into.

Ignorance about wild animals only hurts wild animals. Grizzly, black and polar bears are large, solitary creatures that do not want to be our friends. The best way to decrease the number of bear attacks on humans is for humans to show respect for the animal and for its habitat. Bears need to be left alone in the wild with enough undisturbed space to effectively breed and live. Otherwise, clashes between bear and man will only increase.

Cute and cuddly-looking, young cubs bring out irresistible emotions—the urge to approach is hard to overcome. However, sows are very protective of their young, and will attack anything that they consider a threat to their offspring.

BEAR VS. MAN

Around noon on May 21, 1999, Glenda Ann Bradley, a school teacher, and her former husband, Ralph Hill, entered Great Smoky Mountain National Park for an enjoyable day of hiking and fishing. Having been to the park several times, Hill knew the better places to fish and suggested they walk two miles up the Little River trailhead in Elkmont, Tennessee, and spend the afternoon. It was supposed to be a lazy day full of fishing, lounging in the grass, napping and enjoying the abundant scenery. However, neither of them was aware that a malnourished black bear with a hungry cub were in the area and looking for food.

At about 2 p.m., Ralph Hill hiked up the trail to fish, while Glenda Ann Bradley sat and waited along the Little River trail for him to return. Hill fished a familiar island area for about an hour and then decided to return. When he got back to where he had last seen Glenda, she was missing.

Great Smoky Mountain National Park is easy to get lost in — it is heavily wooded with thick vegetation. Thinking Glenda had to be nearby, Hill searched the area and eventually found her day pack near where she had been sitting earlier. Starting to worry, he broadened his search and then spotted two bears — a 112-pound female (35-pounds underweight) and a 40-pound cub — standing over Glenda's lifeless body. Unable to scare off the aggressive bears, Hill went to find help and around 5 p.m., he ran into another hiker. He told him what had happened and asked him to run to the Elkmont campground and notify park rangers. By 6:05 p.m., rangers arrived at the scene and found the two bears feeding on the victim's body. Both bears were immediately shot and killed. Unofficial policy is that when a predacious bear kills a human and then feeds on the body, it is immediately destroyed.

There was no witness to the attack. The details of how Bradley reacted when she encountered the black bears is not known. Did she see the bear coming and try to defend herself? Did she drop her pack hoping the bears would be content to rummage through its contents, giving her the time to escape and find help? When it attacked, did she fight or play dead? We don't know the answers. It is known, however, that the mother black bear acted aggressively towards officials when they arrived at the scene. Obviously, she had lost her fear of humans, probably accustomed to their presence in the park. When park rangers arrived, the bear bluff charged, snapped its jaws defiantly, and slapped the ground in front of her in a defensive manner. A bear defending a pig or deer carcass will act the same way. The sow clearly considered Bradley prey, regarding her as a food source and teaching her cub this lesson.

Bradley died of blood loss from the bear mauling and her death was ruled accidental by the park service. A few weeks after the attack, an autopsy was done on the bears, confirming that they had fed on Bradley's body, giving park rangers good reason to kill them. Officials believe it is the first recorded human death from a black bear in the southeastern United States.

According to Great Smoky Mountain National Park wildlife biologist, Kim Delozier, the sow had been tagged in 1988 by University of Tennessee wildlife researchers. The sow did not have a history of being a problem bear. The bear never touched Bradley's day pack, which had food in it. In most cases, a food-conditioned or experienced bear would have smelled the food inside the pack and eaten its contents. This black bear went straight for Bradley and ignored the day pack placed close beside her on the ground. Perhaps the bear was startled by Glenda Bradley and attacked her in defense of herself and her cub first. Then, only after the attack began, did the bears start to feed on her body. Without a witness, it is impossible to determine what happened in this bear/human encounter. Regardless, the outcome is tragic, both for Glenda Bradley and for the bears.

Normally, black bears do not stalk and eat humans. However, a stalking black bear is extremely dangerous. If a bear acts or looks like it is stalking you, find shelter immediately — without running — and do not climb a tree! Black bears are excellent tree climbers and will climb right after you. Also, do not play dead! Playing dead will usually stop a grizzly bear attack, but not a black bear attack. However, if either species views you as prey rather than as a threat, fight back.

No one knows exactly why a bear quits viewing humans as a threat to run from and starts to see them as prey to hunt. Shortages of food certainly change their attitudes, causing them to become belligerent towards people, especially if they are already seasoned to humans. A bear's experiences throughout its life finding food and interacting with its environment may provide the best answers. If a bear smells food — if it doesn't already know better — it will investigate the source of the odor. If it is rewarded with food when it arrives, its desire to get to more food overwhelms its shyness, causing it to become bolder and more aggressive with each reward. The bear that attacked Bradley may have been conditioned to human garbage, or at least familiar with human presence in the park.

At roughly 2 p.m. on November 1, 1999, hunters Gene Moe, 68, armed with a seven-inch knife, and Ned Rasmussen, 53, armed with a .270 rifle, were both brutally attacked by giant brown bears 15 miles apart on the Kodiak archipelago in Alaska. Only one survived to tell his story.

In 1999 on the Kodiak archipelago, deep snow covered the landscape into late spring. The snow discouraged new grass shoots, one of the bears' favorite spring food sources. Later in the summer, the berry crop was poor and the salmon runs were low. Bears were nervous and fidgety, wandering hungry, looking for food anywhere they could find it. One source became the black-tail deer shot by hunters. Due to the harsh winter, thirty percent of the blacktail deer herd, transplanted to Kodiak in the 1950s for sport hunting, died. Brown bears used to salmon feasts and fields of lush green grass were now starving and they started to become unusually aggressive towards humans.

The bears had learned that a gunshot meant food, and began interpreting the sound as a dinner invitation. In the fall of 1999, the Alaska Department of Fish and Game warned deer hunters to hunt only in pairs, advising that one hunter should butcher the game while the other stood guard and watched for bears, keeping a gun close. It was a long and emotional season for Sergeant Darlene Turner, a state trooper and coordinator for Kodiak's Search and Rescue.

"Last year there was a real need to be more bear aware," Turner said. "Everything was late and the bears were hungry. People are not mad at the bears for what happened. That is not the issue. The issue is a hunter made a mistake and it cost him his life, which is just an incredible tragedy. Everything that could go wrong did go wrong."

Hunting alone turned out to be a fatal mistake for Ned Rasmussen. An experienced outdoorsman, Rasmussen was used to bears backing off when he encountered them. He had hunted in the Kodiak area for 15 years without any problems, and he intimately knew the landscape. For him, seeing bears was commonplace. But in November of 1999, he was reported missing by the other members of his hunting party.

"People here are tough. We do about ten to twenty searches a year for missing people, mostly during the hunting season," Turner said. "Rasmussen obviously had a lot of [outdoor] skills, but unfortunately none of them prepared him for what happened."

The Coast Guard picked up an emergency signal at 12:30 p.m. on November 2. They dispatched two HH-60 helicopters and one C-130 airplane to search the area. They scoured the vicinity, flying low patterns over Uganik Island. At about 3:40 p.m., one of the helicopter crews spotted a three-man hunting party near a remote cabin on the west side of the island. They landed, picked up one of the hunters and then continued searching well into the night for Rasmussen, using sophisticated Forward Looking Infrared Radar (FLIR), a heat-sensing device. The helicopter crew spotted a piece of paper wrapped around an alder bush. It looked as if someone had placed it there to mark the location to be able to find it later. The crew hovered over the area when suddenly, out of a thick alder patch, a giant brown bear charged, challenging the helicopter. It seemed like it was almost going to jump inside, according to one crew member. The bear eventually ran back into the thicket. At 7 p.m., Alaska state troopers and Kodiak Island Search and Rescue joined the search at the scene but they found nothing that evening.

Tuesday morning the search resumed with the aid of search dogs. The crew landed and began scouring the area where the bear had charged the helicopter previously. Upon further inspection, they found a bloodied hat, drag marks with blood, and about fifty feet away, an empty rifle with bear hair on the end of the barrel. Clearly, something terrible had happened.

Separating from his three hunting companions, Ned Rasmussen, backpack loaded with hunting gear, decided to hunt a different area. He knew deer numbers were low and thought his best chance to shoot a buck was to hunt a familiar ridge, a site he had hunted several times.

In an interview with state troopers, one of Ned's hunting partners stated that he had heard a gun shot, looked up on a distant hill and saw Rasmussen. He tried to signal him but he was too far away, and Rasmussen disappeared along the trail over the ridge. A little while later, the hunter was glassing the same hill when he spotted a big bear on the north side of the hill, walking around and heading towards the area he had just seen Ned.

"Generally, Kodiak's brown bears don't like confrontations with people and almost always, given the opportunity, will give ground," Turner said. "We have some bears the size of buffalos on the island. Just last week I watched a ten-and-a-half foot, 1400- to 1800-pound brown bear walk out of the forest. There were eight other bears there and as soon as they saw the big one, they immediately ran off."

Two hours after hearing the first shot, Rasmussen's hunting companions heard him shoot again. They simply thought he had shot at another deer, as hunters are allowed to shoot five deer a year on Kodiak. It wasn't until later that they found out it was not another deer. No one will ever know the details about Rasmussen's last hours, how he killed the deer, left it and walked off for two hours. However, the attack site did reveal what happened when he returned.

According to reports, Rasmussen had butchered the deer,

left it where it was shot, and walked around the hill. Two hours later he came back and found a brown bear had taken possession of the carcass. The bear must have charged Rasmussen, who was able to fire his .270 caliber rifle, the second shot his companions heard. Rasmussen had placed a piece of white medical tape over the end of his rifle barrel to prevent debris from getting into and plugging the barrel. When searchers found the rifle, fifty feet from the attack site, dark brown bear hair was stuck to the tape, indicating that the bear literally ran into Rasmussen's rifle when it charged. The small caliber rifle didn't stop the bear. The bear immediately attacked, biting him in the shoulder and the hip, shaking him violently and dropping him. Later, the autopsy revealed that Rasmussen suffered massive internal injuries caused by severe blows. His hip and shoulder were crushed. There were also skin-deep bite marks above his eyebrows and at the base of his skull on the opposite side, indicating that it was a huge bear, probably a boar. Once Rasmussen quit fighting and played dead, the bear went back to feeding on the deer. Rasmussen, bleeding heavily, crawled down the hill about three to four-hundred yards where he died from loss of blood. There was no indication the bear followed him after it attacked.

The dog teams and searchers found a blood trail leading away from the attack site. They followed it, eventually finding Rasmussen's body. There was no indication of predation. Because of the steep terrain where he was found, a helicopter was summoned and Rasmussen was placed on a stretcher and transported to Kodiak.

The same day a bear was seen by the crew of the helicopter. The bear appeared to have a fresh blood wound on its shoulder as it charged out of an alder patch. They chose not to destroy it.

Fifteen miles away on Raspberry Island, in the same hour that Rasmussen was attacked, Gene Moe was also fighting for his life.

"I've had a lot of bear trouble . . . lots of trouble," Moe remembers. "In fact, I like a cockroach better than a bear. Years ago I shot and killed a bear with a shotgun as it crashed through a cabin window where my wife was staying. In the 50s, I saved a guy who was charged by a grizzly and luckily hit it in the neck just before it got him. Once, I kicked a black bear and . . . I thought they were a joke; I won't do that again. Since I have lived in Alaska I've had eight friends killed by bears . . . . Like I said, lots of trouble."

"Last year I was gutting a deer on Kodiak Island and a bear came, stood up and chattered his teeth. I said 'Bear, you can have it!' It picked the deer up like a cat carries a kitten and walked off."

Moe vividly recalls the day he was attacked on Kodiak Island in 1999.

"The day I was attacked I was alone hunting near Selief Creek on Raspberry Island, in heavy woods and ah . . . there was another thing I didn't want to believe, but I believe now. In Kodiak country, when the bears hear a [gun] shot, they think it's food for them and they come running."

"I waited about ten minutes after I shot the deer and there was no bear. There was no way that I could carry it out to a better opening so I placed my rifle down close by and started to butcher the deer. Thirty minutes later, I heard a sound, looked up, and the bear came at me growling and snapping its teeth."

At the time, Moe didn't realize there was a habituated bear in the area. The day before Moe was attacked, guide Tom Stick, from Kodiak, reported that a large bear with two cubs had come into their camp along the Selief River and had gotten into their garbage. The cubs climbed a tree with a garbage bag and ripped it open, spilling its contents on the ground and eating what was left.

"An old male bear will come in and cuff you around a bit and then leave," Moe recalled the day of his attack. "This bear came in biting. This bear didn't come to maul me, it came to kill me. It bit me in my arm just above the elbow and then it took a huge chunk out of my leg. But that bear couldn't take it as good as it dished it out. When I grabbed my 7-inch folding buck knife and started stabbing it in the throat and I buried my finger in its ear, then it was a different story. He didn't like that very much."

"I will tell you something about bears you probably don't know. If I see a bear charging with both feet at the same time, straight ahead, he's coming in to kill me. If the bear comes in one foot at a time, he's going to stop, stand up and chatter his teeth, and then probably leave if you stand your ground. I'll tell you something else about bears: all bears are right handed. I knew this when the brown bear attacked me. The next time you see a bear, watch it and see which paw it uses to bring food to its mouth. If I wouldn't have known that, the bear would have killed me."

"When the bear came at me the second time, I wasn't watching him, I was watching his right paw. As soon as he moved it to strike, I leaned my head back and he missed. If I hadn't moved he would have taken my head clean off."

"The bear knocked me down and I started kicking it with both legs in the head and neck. It backed off for a minute and gave me time to get up. The third time he came in, I knew I was in trouble. The bear was doing too much damage. I had to do something. So, when the right paw came, I stepped to the side and thrust the knife deep into its neck. That's when he bit me again on the leg. I wrenched the knife and grabbed him around the neck trying to break him down like a wrestler you see on television, but of course he was too strong and he flipped me about six feet into the air. He backed off for a second and started to leave, but came at me again."

"The fourth time he charged his mouth was frothing blood and his head was crooked on an angle. I also was bleeding badly and getting tired. When the bear lunged the last time, I hit him as hard as I could with my fist. The blow must have hurt his neck and he backed away."

Moe grabbed his rifle and fired, hitting the bear in the chest just as it charged again. The shot killed the bear almost instantly and it collapsed in a heap of fur and blood.

"That was the toughest day of my life. Right after the attack I crawled two miles to reach safety, up and down hills," Moe said.

Upon reaching his hunting companions, they took Moe to a nearby lodge, cleaned him up the best they could and called for help. A United States Coast Guard helicopter carried him out of the area to Kodiak. When he arrived at the hospital, doctors placed over two-hundred stitches to repair his battered body. He was missing ten pounds of muscle from his leg and bones were protruding from his elbow and were skinned clear to his hands. He was lucky to be alive.

"That bear was just hungry," Moe said. "Not a bit of fat on it."

The scenario is happening all too often on Kodiak Island. A hunter kills a deer. A bear is hungry, hears the gunshot, and thinks dinner is served.

A press release by the Department of Fish and Game dated November 4, 1999 stated: *Wildlife Officials urge all sportsmen to use extreme caution while in the field on the Kodiak archipelago. There have been four Kodiak bears killed while they charged hunters and two hunters attacked, one fatally. . . . Compounding the problem is the reduced deer population. Fewer deer mean that hunters have to spend more time in the field looking for their prey, ultimately increasing their chances of running into a bear. The bears they do encounter may be less tolerant than usual.*

The seven hundred pound brown bear that attacked Gene Moe was thin, starving, and was estimated to be 12 years old. Ned Rasmussen was attacked and killed by another hungry brown bear only fifteen miles away. However, the State Fish and Game department concluded that the low salmon numbers were not to blame for these attacks, although they did concede that the sparse berry crops could have affected bear behavior. Larry Van Daele, Kodiak's wildlife biologist with the state Fish and Game, investigated Moe's attack. A portion of his report follows and has been edited slightly.

Mr. Moe's son brought the bear hide into our office about a week after the incident. They found her at the site of the mauling along with her two cubs (about 135 pounds each) who scattered as they approached. The hide was salted when they brought it in with the head and paws intact. There were three wounds that I could find: one in the chest area, one in the neck and one in the throat. The throat wound was the only one that did any notable damage, cutting an arteriole and severing part of a lingual ligament. There was also an older wound on the top of its head which was a round puncture. The wound did not puncture the skull, but was a subdermal contusion about seven centimeters in diameter. Blood in the nose and mouth suggested the bear died rapidly from a heart/lung shot.

Van Daele stated, " . . . the berry crop was a huge failure last year. Salmon numbers had nothing to do with the attacks. In fact, salmon numbers are normal to high in most places. The late season, combined with cold weather, killed the berry crop and the plants redirected their energy to growing leaves and vines instead of producing berries. Bears rely on berries as a fall food source. Bears are predictable in most instances. In the fall they are looking for a last shot of food before entering the den and if they can't find it, we have problems."

"Gene Moe and Ned Rasmussen broke the rules. They hunted alone in a country filled with over 3,000 of the world's largest brown bears. The bears are just doing what comes naturally to them . . . looking for food."

The leading cause of death among "teenage" polar bears is starvation. And if you asked 66-year-old native, Moses Aliyak, he would probably say a starving polar bear is the most dangerous animal in the world — he has been attacked by them twice.

Mother polar bears kick their young out when the cubs are two-and-a-half years old, sometime in the spring just before the sows come into estrus. The cubs have been with their mother since they were born, never leaving her protection for long. When their mother turns on them, swatting and chasing them away, it is hard on the young bears and they are unwilling to leave. Eventually, her persistence wins and the cubs head off into the white arctic. They are completely alone and must fend for themselves. Most become scavengers at first, eating leftover seal carcasses, robbing birds' nests and, sometimes, finding people's garbage. They are always hungry, following their keen noses as they wander the ice pack in search of food. It is this empty belly that usually leads them into trouble.

In July of 1994, Moses Aliyak and his family were at their hunting camp getting ready for a caribou hunt. Moses was busy rounding up supplies outside while his wife was inside preparing food for the hunt. Suddenly, without warning, Moses found himself faced with a defensive mother polar bear and her two bawling cubs. The sow reared up on her hind legs, towering feet over Moses' head, and placed her massive paws on his shoulders ready to bite him. Moses remembered what his ancestors had taught him about polar bears not turning their heads to bite something long and slender. He raised his arm to a ninety degree angle and placed it in front of the bear's mouth. It worked! She didn't bite his arm as the two started to wrestle. Moses reached down and grabbed the bear's leg and pulled upwards as hard as he could. At the same time, amazingly, the polar bear fell backwards as she must have been off-balance. When she landed on the ground, the surprised sow stared at Moses, not understanding what had happened and seemingly unsure of what to do next. Moses simply stared back, waiting. The bear suddenly turned and ran off with her cubs

Although Moses was unharmed in this first encounter, the next time he, and others, were not so fortunate.

The headline of the *Nunatsiaq News* in the Northwest Territories read: "Polar Bear Kills One, Injures Two Others." The attack took place while Margaret Amarook, 56, the step-daughter of Hattie Amitnaag, 64, was fetching water at a nearby spring. Hattie and her grandson, Eddie, were left at camp and were inside the tent. Moses and his grandson, Cyrus, had gone to catch their boat that had drifted away earlier in the day.

"I had taken the five gallon barrel to fetch some water," said Amarook. "The water canteen was very heavy so I had my head down." As she carried the water back to camp, she noticed that she didn't hear the others. As she looked around, everything seemed quiet, dangerously quiet, and she hurried back to camp. She did not know that at that moment Moses was being attacked by a hungry six-foot polar bear.

Moses and his grandson, Cyrus, were the first to encounter the bear.

"Our boat had gone adrift with all our gear, guns and harpoons, everything on board," Aliyak said. "As the bear approached, I knew I was going to be able to fight it, but I also knew I had to steer it away from the tent."

Moses ran away from the tent hoping the bear would give chase and follow him, which it did. As he ran, Moses bent over and picked up a softball-sized rock, thinking that he would step to the side when the bear got close enough, and then strike the bear's head as it ran past. Just before the bear reached him, however, Moses tripped over a stone and fell to the ground. Off balance, he still tried to hit the bear with the rock, but missed, hitting its nose with his forearm instead. The polar bear grabbed his arm and began to shake him violently. Moses was helpless.

"I was supposed to be the one protecting my grandchildren and those in our camp," Moses regretfully said later.

After the young bear finished attacking and severely mauling Moses, it turned toward the hunting tent just as Hattie and Eddie, Moses' 10-year-old grandson, walked out of the tent. They bravely tried to run to try and help Moses, but they didn't get far. The bear stopped and looked at them, giving Moses time to run and hide in a broken down cabin close to the tent.

At this point, Margaret Amarook walked on the scene.

"The bear was in front of the tent and there was blood on the tent," Amarook said. "I could not see what it was eating. I dropped the water and just stood there." She watched Moses walk from behind the shack and move closer to the tent. He had been severely mauled. He was bleeding profusely from his head, and it looked as if he was missing an eye and part of his nose was gone.

The polar bear then charged Hattie and Eddie, attacking the little boy first. It viciously bit at his head and neck area, and finally swiped him with a powerful forepaw that knocked him unconscious. Hattie screamed and tried to distract the bear. The bear then went after her.

The elderly woman put up a courageous fight against the bear. Her dentures were found in one place and her wrist watch in another. However, the bear was too powerful and it killed Hattie in a ferocious attack.

While Hattie was being mauled, Amarook ran to Moses and told him to stay there and she went for help. David and Rosie

Oolooyuk's hunting camp was nearby and she used their two-way radio to call the community of Rankin Inlet.

Helicopter pilot Daniel Kennedy was the first to arrive on scene.

"On July 9, about 3 p.m., we received a call at the hanger from the RMCP [Royal Canadian Mounted Police] requesting helicopter support for a possible bear attack," Kennedy said. "When we arrived on the scene, it was decided that I was to get out with a shotgun with rifle slugs and clear the area, making sure it was okay for everybody else. The first thing we saw was a young Inuit boy . . . waving from the tent, and we put the helicopter down and I jumped out with the 12-gauge [shotgun]. He [Cyrus] met me halfway and I asked if he was okay and he said 'Yes,' and then pointed back behind him and he said, 'Those two people are dead.'"

Kennedy could see that Hattie was obviously dead, as she had been skinned from the shoulders down. Kennedy also saw a young boy crumpled over into a small ball, with his legs apart and his head almost touching his right knee. The boy looked dead, sitting in an unnatural position.

"He looked as if he had been crushed from above. He had bad lacerations on the back of his head and neck," Kennedy recalled. When he reached to check for a pulse, the boy said, "Ow! Don't touch my head." Luckily, Eddie was still alive, although in pretty bad shape.

The family was flown to Ranking Inlet by Helicopter for medical care. Although scarred physically, both Moses and Eddie survived the ordeal. Meanwhile, rescuers and other officials pieced together what had happened, and figured out where the bear had come from and where it had gone.

The young polar bear approached the campsite from the water — tracks were found near the shoreline. Gerald Fillatre, the investigating wildlife officer with the Renewable Resources Department, stated that he believed the bear had just been kicked out by its mother and probably had just started hunting on its own. On the shoreline, researchers found remains of an old caribou kill and human garbage scattered about. Bite marks revealed the bear had eaten the contents of some tin cans and, later, its tracks lead toward the tent where it first attacked Moses.

Because the bear seemed to be human-conditioned and because it had attacked its victims without being provoked, the officials decided to find the polar bear and kill it before it found another camp and attacked others. Within half an hour after taking off in the helicopter, they spotted a bear almost two miles away from the campsite. They hovered over it, shot and killed it, assuming it was the animal responsible for the attacks. An autopsy revealed that the bear had eaten human flesh, confirming their conclusion. Hattie Amitnaag was the first polar bear inflicted death in Canada in twenty years.

Although this attack occurred in a remote location in Canada to native residents, the danger is not as distant as it might appear. As the popularity of eco-tourism expands to include faraway places, people in search of adventurous experiences are encountering polar bears. Polar bears are dangerous, but statistically they rarely kill humans. The low chance of encountering a polar bear has a lot to do with the low number of attacks, however. Polar bears live isolated, nomadic lives, only venturing close to human encampments when absolutely necessary or if they are drawn by human refuse. As humans venture closer to their domain, however, it is only reasonable to assume that attacks by polar bears on humans will become more common.

ATTACKS: ARE THEY INCREASING?

BEAR VS. MAN
162

PHOTOGRAPHING BEARS

In order to take quality photographs of bears in the wild, your choice of camera gear is important to be able to stay a safe distance away from the animal. I won't go into the details of different camera brands and the functions of each, but the following are the basics of camera gear for photographing bears. (Much of what I discuss is directed toward serious amateurs or those who would like to be professional photographers. Snapshots taken with an automatic 35mm can be just as rewarding, just keep your distance.)

You will need a 35mm SLR (single lens reflex) camera, at least a 400mm (equivalent to 8 power) telephoto lens, and a sturdy tripod or some type of support.

SLR's are the camera of choice for professional photographers because of their flexibility and interchangeable lenses. Today's auto-focus SLRs are highly sophisticated, easy-to-use cameras that allow beginners to take professional-quality pictures with just a push of the button. They are as simple as focus, compose and shoot.

A good place to compare cameras is the Internet; advice from professional photographers and information in magazines like *Shutterbug*, *Popular Photography* and *Outdoor Photographer* are also good resources. Look for camera body reviews that interest you and see what brands professionals are using. Take a trip to your local camera store and peruse the different brands of camera bodies. Hold the camera in your hand and look for fit, functionality, and the features that are most important to you, such as auto-focus, frames per second, number of program modes and, most importantly, interchangeable lenses and a wide assortment of focal lengths. All major camera manufacturers provide an array of different focal lengths.

LENSES

The most important piece of equipment is the lens. It is also the item you should not skimp on. When professional photographers are asked what is the most important piece of equipment in their arsenal of camera gear, they say their lenses. The sharpness of images is dictated by lens quality.

Higher power lenses like 800mm (equivalent to 16 power) have advantages and disadvantages, but be ready with a deep wallet or credit card. Large, fast lenses are expensive. Good glass is costly to produce but it provides superior image quality and has greater light gathering capabilities. Also, their excellent magnification means the larger the image in the viewfinder. This allows you the luxury of keeping a safe distance from the bear rather than using a smaller lens and having to get closer to a dangerous situation.

Do your homework when deciding which lens to buy. Stay in the 400mm range and higher, knowing that the more powerful the better. Get the fastest (lowest aperture number, meaning it gathers more light enabling faster shutter speeds) lens you can afford. If you're considering selling your images, do not rely on the price as the most important factor when making your decision. In the long run, you will be happier with a better-quality lens and it will save you the hassle of trying to unload used camera gear when you decide to upgrade to better equipment (which is inevitable). The adage "you get what you pay for" is definitely true when it comes to camera lenses.

TRIPODS

The key to a good tripod is its sturdiness. When you are looking for a sturdy tripod, fully extend the legs and twist the tripod by grabbing the top. If it moves more than two inches in either direction, you should consider purchasing a firmer tripod. Super-telephoto lenses are heavier than smaller lenses and require heavy tripods, which are normally sturdier but seem to get heavier with each step when hiking rugged terrain. The new graphite series by Gitzo are ideal for hiking and lugging around. They are light and extremely sturdy, but they are also more expensive. You will need to find a balance between rigidity and weight when selecting the right tripod that fits your pocketbook.

THE SHOT

The demand by magazine editors' for bears showing their bad dental hygiene seems to be today's norm, but these images portray a false image of bears and actually do bears a disservice. How do photographers get these unnatural shots? The answer is game farms. These rent-an-animal-for-a-day farms are specifically designed to cater to photographers who are after close-ups of bears and other hard to find, let alone photograph, wildlife. For an hourly or per day fee, you can chose from a wide variety of animals including cougars, wolves, wolverines, and other elusive critters. Chances are if you see a magazine cover with an irate looking grizzly on it, it probably was taken at a game farm. How can you tell? Make a mental record of the bear's facial features, coat marks or broken teeth. Then, the next time you see another cover of a similar grizzly, look to see if it has the same features as the previous bear. If it does, there is a good chance the bear was photographed at a game farm. The most popular "cover bear" has a broken front canine and has appeared on many national magazine covers.

Even Hollywood's most famous bear, Bart, the star of several movies like *The Edge* and *The Bear*, is trained to stand on a "point" rock and roar at the cameraman. Photographers move into position as the ten-foot-tall hulk stands and they fire frame after frame of opened-mouthed portraits. In the wild, bears don't waste time with these gestures. When they mean business, bears charge in and attack.

If you need bear photos and don't mind shooting captive animals, game farms are a sure and reasonably safe way to build your inventory and get some great images. But, if you are looking for adrenaline-pumping, heart-pounding action outdoors, photograph wild bears.

Bear photography provides hours and sometimes days of boredom mixed with seconds of extreme excitement. There are other times when the action is non-stop and you just cannot run enough film though your camera. Although frustrating at times, photographing bears in the wild is usually very rewarding.

BEST TIMES TO PHOTOGRAPH BEARS

Spring and fall are the best times to photograph bears. In the spring, bears have full coats of hair while fall bears have shorter hair but heavier bodies, a result of the summer's feeding frenzy. Bears emerge from their dens sometime in March to April depending on location, weather, and how they fared through the winter. The healthier they are when they enter the den generally the earlier they leave to begin searching for food. Mothers

with cubs leave the den later than single bears. Cubs are born in January and are still too small to travel and keep up with their mother.

Bears are the most active during the morning and evening hours. Midday hours are spent sleeping beneath a cool shade tree or lounging near a stream. In hot weather, bears only move when necessary to find a cooler spot to sleep until evening, sometimes preferring the shady, dark timber beds pine trees provide. Try to stay in the open when hiking in bear country rather than through these timber patches. Surprising a sleeping bear can turn ugly, fast. The first and last few hours of the day are the best times for bear photography. When the sun is lower in the horizon it generates a softer light that produces better pictures.

BEST PLACES TO PHOTOGRAPH BEARS

Alaska is the best place to see wild bears. Its diverse habitats and large population provide ample opportunities to see wild bears. Not necessarily in any order, below are the top places to see bears along with the best times to visit.

KATMAI NATIONAL PARK, ALASKA

Located 300 miles southwest of Anchorage, Katmai National Park is a land of rivers, glaciers, mountainous terrain and home to an estimated 2,000 brown bears. Brooks River Falls is the center of bear activity and the best times to visit it coincide with the salmon run.

Each year, about mid-July, thousands of sockeye salmon swim upstream to fight their way over natural obstacles and past patient bears that anchor themselves at the cornice of Brooks River Falls. The salmon jump up the three-foot hurdle. Some make it, and others end up in the paws of a hungry bear.

Two bear-viewing platforms are located along Brooks River:

A ranger watches from the deck as a brown bear looks for fish at Brooks River Falls in Alaska.

one deck is at the falls and the other is close to the lodge, about 300 yards away. Both are great places to see brown bears, provided the bears are awake and moving. There are a lot of bears

Being in the right place at the right time is critical to photographing bears.
These Katmai National Park cubs pose a moment for the camera.

here and they can appear anywhere, so have your camera loaded with film and be ready for action.

To get to Katmai, visitors must first fly to Anchorage and then either rent a car or book a flight to Homer. Once there, the last leg of the journey involves a scenic, 20-minute floatplane ride from King Salmon to Brooks River Falls.

Advanced reservations are required and may be acquired through the National Park Reservation Service at 1-800-365-

2267 or (international) 1-301-722-1257. They recommend calling at least three weeks before your planned visit. For more information visit their website at <www.nps.gov/katm/>.

McNeil River Sanctuary, Alaska

Considered by many to be one of the greatest wonders of the world, McNeil River Sanctuary in Alaska is truly a destination for young aspiring bear photographers. Visitors to this special place must be adventurous and self-sufficient. Bears here are accustomed to humans and will come extremely close. It is wise to stay in well-defined viewing areas. Bring plenty of film and be prepared to shoot it. Bears can be behind every bush and seen in and around camp to the McNeil River Falls, where it is thought that the largest brown bears in the world gather to fish for spawning salmon.

A permit system and user fees are required by the Alaska Department of Fish & Game to visit the sanctuary. At the time of this writing, the deadline to apply for a permit is March 1 and winners are selected by random drawing. Lucky individuals who acquire a permit will spend four fantastic days photographing and enjoying McNeil's free ranging brown bears. It is, without a doubt, bears at their best.

The peak time to visit is middle to late July when visitors can expect to see 30 or more wild bears at the falls and 100 or so coming and going around the area. For more information, contact Alaska Department of Fish & Game at 1-907-267-2182 or visit their website at <www.state.ak.us/local/akpages/FISH.GAME/> and follow the links to Refuges, Critical Habitat Areas and Sanctuaries until you see McNeil River.

To get there, fly into Anchorage and head south towards Homer. From there, numerous floatplane providers can fly you the rest of the way to McNeil for a reasonable fee.

Denali National Park in Alaska is a great place to see the Toklat grizzly bear. School buses are used to transport tourists into its backcountry.

DENALI NATIONAL PARK, ALASKA

Among deep, picturesque valleys and snow-covered peaks towering over 20,000 feet above sea level lies the heart of Alaska: Denali National Park. Home to a small population of black bears and 200 to 300 grizzly bears (sometimes referred as Toklat grizzlies), Denali is a massive and irresistibly beautiful park. It is prime habitat for the grizzly bear and is generally considered by professional photographers to be the best place in Alaska to photograph interior grizzlies. Along with Denali's bears are opportunities to photograph wild sheep, moose, caribou, and other native Alaskan animals around each bend or over the next hill.

Depending on your choice of habitat coloration, the best time to visit is either June or August. In the spring, vegetation is lush and green as bears dig for plant roots. They can be found wandering on the treeless open tundra. Fall weather brings a mosaic pattern of oranges, reds and yellows that look as if a painter has wildly splashed the vivid colors across the tundra. Bears can be seen aimlessly wandering across this canvas of colors and sometimes come close enough for a picture. If you have a big lens, bring it. Park rangers strictly enforce the rules of not approaching bears on foot.

Denali is a five-hour drive north of Anchorage. Upon your arrival in the park, it is recommended to go straight to the visitors' center and apply for the next day's bus permit. Get the earliest trip possible. You will need the bus ticket to pass through the gate at the end of a 15 mile paved road and to enter the 85-mile gravel road that winds deep into the park. Visit <http://www.nps.gov/dena/> or call the park service at 1-907-683-2294 for more details.

Yellowstone National Park, Wyoming

The oldest national park can also be the hottest or coldest park for bear viewing. Although both black and grizzly bears can be seen regularly in Yellowstone's Lamar Valley, they are usually distant specks and are only discernible with high-power spotting scopes. If you are hoping to get closer to a Yellowstone bear, you will need a lot of patience and time. Days and gas tanks can be spent driving around looking for bears near or along the many roads. Despite their obvious inconvenience, consider yourself lucky if you happen upon one of Yellowstone's infamous "bear jams." Although bears are common in the park's backcountry, they have been trained by park rangers to stay away from roads and people.

Yellowstone National Park is located in the northwest corner of Wyoming. There are several ways to enter the park, the most popular being through West Yellowstone, Montana. Anytime is a good time to visit the park, but be prepared for crowds as it is a very popular destination.

The morning fog lifts inside Yellowstone National Park

In early June, Lamar Valley is a great place to find wolves and bears chasing elk calves born to anxious mothers. Seasonal hot spots to see grizzly bears are Pahaska Tepee, just outside the park on the road to Cody, Wyoming, and around Tower Junction where black bears prefer the thicker, rougher terrain. Bears are active in the early morning and evening hours so adjust your itinerary accordingly. For up to date information, visit: <http://www.nps.gov/yell/> or visit their expanded website at <http://www.nps.gov/yell/home.htm> or phone 1-307-344-7381.

GLACIER NATIONAL PARK, MONTANA

Glacier National Park has been described as the Crowning Jewel of the North American continent. It is also a hikers' and bears' paradise. Over 700 miles of both rugged and easy trails take the backcountry visitor past grizzly and black bears, bighorn sheep, mountain goats, elk, mule deer and a host of other wildlife. It is a harsh yet thrilling environment.

Glacier's bears have the reputation of being particularly ornerier than Alaska's bears. Sow grizzlies are extremely protective of their cubs and do not tolerate surprises or threats from humans. Bear maulings or killings are not unheard of in Glacier's backcountry. Be especially careful around Glacier's bears and make them aware of your presence.

An estimated 250 to 400 grizzlies live within the park's boundaries, with roughly the same number of black bears. Bears can be seen along Going-to-the-Sun road as they devour the lush green vegetation against the backdrop of Glacier's breathtaking waterfalls. Going-to-the-Sun road hugs the cliff below the Continental Divide and winds its way toward Logan Pass at 6,646 feet above sea level. Vehicle road restrictions apply to the pass road, so be sure to check with the park service before you visit.

Unfortunately, Glacier's interior is weather dependent, but the rest of the park is open year-round, 24 hours a day. Visit Glacier's official website at <http://www.nps.gov/glac/> or call 1-406-888-7800 for more trip information.

BANFF NATIONAL PARK, ALBERTA, CANADA

A photographer's paradise, Banff National Park is Canada's oldest and most famous park, and is home to grizzlies, mountain goats and some of North America's wildest creatures. The five million visitors a year who travel to Banff never quite know where they will run into one of the park's estimated 100 bears

A tourist photographs bear cubs inside Yellowstone National Park

(70 grizzly and 30 black bears). The Bow Valley Parkway, Ice Fields Parkway, or Bow Summit areas are great bear habitat and good places to find both grizzly and black bears.

Banff's bears usually don't emerge from their slumber until late April or early May, and can generally be seen up until early October. Spring brings a splash of yellow dandelions and new shoots of grass along the roadsides that attract the bears. During the fall, bears move higher up the mountains in search of berries, making a sighting along the roadside rarer. The bears here are used to cars and people so be extra careful as you take pictures. Stay in your car if the bear is within 100 yards and use a window mount or bean bag to support your camera.

Banff is located 80 miles west of Calgary along the Trans-Canada Highway (#1). There is an international airport in Calgary and buses run year-round to and from the park. If you continue west another 180 miles you will reach the town of Jasper, which is less crowded and more isolated than Banff.

For more information about Banff National Park, visit their website at <www.worldweb.com/ParksCanada-Banff/> or call 1-403-762-1550 and ask for an information packet.

JASPER NATIONAL PARK, ALBERTA, CANADA

This is the largest national park in Canada and the most northerly of the four connected Canadian Rocky Mountain parks: Banff, Yoho, Kootenay and Jasper. It is stunningly rugged and is one of my favorite national parks to photograph for both wildlife and scenics. Bull elk run through campgrounds in the fall, bugling their challenge to any and all, sometimes even fighting amongst wide-eyed campers watching from the safety of their vehicles or camp trailers. Granite peaks jet straight up and then vertically drop thousands of feet to turquoise blue lakes where osprey dive from the sky searching for fish.

Wildlife watching is excellent and often abundant along many of the park's roads. A good place to see bears foraging for spring grasses is along Maligne Road to Medicine and Maligne Lake. Another great place to see wildlife, especially bears, is along Highway 93A, which parallels Highway 93.

There are more than 1,700 campsites in Jasper, offering various levels of service; some are equipped with public showers. The best time to visit Jasper is anytime you can get there, with peak season being May through October. Spring is usually better for bears, while fall brings the elk rut, which peaks in the third week of September. Bears are usually at higher elevations during fall months as they search for food in berry patches, one

Canada is still a stronghold for free-ranging grizzly bears. But as humans continue to push deeper into Canada's wilderness, its wild bears sometimes push back. Increasing numbers of tourists are attracted by the abundant wildlife and beautiful scenery, such as these mountains in Jasper National Park in Alberta.

of their favorite fall food sources.

Jasper National Park is located 192 miles west of Edmonton, 500 miles northeast of Vancouver, and 256 miles northwest of Calgary. Highway 93 from Banff National Park winds its way up the valley. There are numerous pullouts, campgrounds, and scenic views along the road.

Visit Jasper National Park's website at <www.worldweb .com/ParksCanada-Jasper/> or call 1-780- 852-6176 for travel and visitor information.

CHURCHILL, MANITOBA

Considered by many to be the polar bear capital of the world, Churchill is the best place to see the world's largest land carnivores — the fearless polar bear. Professional photographers, researchers, and eco-tourists have traveled to this remote location for years to study and enjoy the white bears. Each year, starting as early as October, migrant polar bears invade

A polar bear stands to get a look at one of the tundra buggy operators near Churchill, Manitoba in Canada. Polar bears are extremely curious animals.

BEAR VS. MAN

184

Churchill to lazily wander around the outskirts of town waiting for Hudson Bay to freeze over so they can hunt seals on the immense icy landscape. As many as 20-30 polar bears can be seen interacting with each other as they stand on two legs and rock back and forth as if dancing.

There are daily tour groups that lead expeditions out into the frozen world to search for the bears. These can easily be found by any Internet search engine. Plan your trip by booking early; reservations are made sometimes years in advance. Keep in close contact with the tour guide companies; cancellations do happen and sometimes you can get lucky. Churchill is truly a trip of a lifetime that keeps giving long after you return home. It provides a unique opportunity to see polar bears in the wild (as you watch them from the safety of a tundra buggy).

Getting to Churchill is an experience in itself. There are no roads that lead to the town. Instead, the two options are by plane or train, both of which run regularly during the peak bear-viewing season.

If you are planning a trip to Churchill to see the polar bears, bring plenty of 100 ASA or 200 ASA film. The light conditions are fickle and fluctuate from overcast to bright sun. Be prepared for the extreme cold weather too. Temperatures can drop well below freezing in this part of the world and winds can instantly freeze body extremities.

THE DANGERS

As this book has repeatedly discussed, being near bears is dangerous, and therefore, photographing bears is dangerous. I cannot stress enough how important it is for photographers to respect the wildlife they pursue for their own sakes and for the sake of the animals. Stories like the following do not need to happen.

William John Tesinsky, a 38-year-old man from Great Falls,

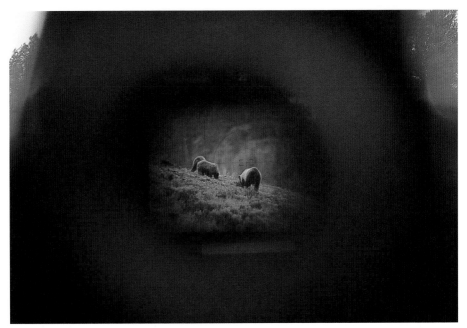

Grizzly bears through the viewfinder.

Montana, knew the dangers of photographing wild bears, but the drive to get close-up grizzly pictures was too strong. He dreamed of becoming a successful wildlife photographer. Earlier, he told his brother that the grizzly bear was the only major animal that he hadn't yet photographed.

While driving north toward Canyon inside Yellowstone National Park, Tesinsky spotted a grizzly feeding in an open and rolling meadow. Grabbing a Pentax 80-200mm zoom lens and a tripod, he parked the car and began following the bear that was about 450 yards from the road. According to accounts of the attack, the wind was probably blowing in Tesinsky's face, covering the sound of his footsteps and definitely his scent, which allowed his approach. The bear moved a short distance to another feeding location as Tesinsky, unaware the bear had moved, continued to move forward.

As Tesinsky topped a small rise, he spotted the adult female grizzly still eating grasses and digging for roots. Judging by his camera setting on the lens (120mm) he set up his tripod 30 to 50 feet away from the bear and prepared to take pictures. The grizzly did not give him the chance. Tesinsky was immediately attacked.

Tesinsky was reported missing late in the afternoon of October 6, 1986. The next morning, two park rangers found the grizzly bear standing guard over Tesinsky's half-consumed body, which she started to drag away as they approached. The bear had to be killed.

Bear photographers do create a management problem for park rangers and wildlife refuge managers. Some photographers — professional and amateur alike — continually push the limits, trying to get close to bears for a frame-filling shot. A well-published Montana photographer deliberately baited grizzlies in order to photograph the bears near his backwoods cabin. The irresponsible photographer was fined, but the damage to the

bears is irreversible. The Shoshone's National Forest Service has just implemented and placed attention-grabbing signs that say anyone who intentionally approaches a bear will be fined $5000. More restrictions on photographing wildlife are sure to follow if photographers do not act responsibly.

If you intend to photograph bears do so responsibly and allow the bear its space. Never pursue or intentionally approach a mother with cubs. Be especially wary of grizzly bears as they are the most dangerous animals to photograph. Watch the bear for warning signs that indicate it feels stress or has a change in attitude toward your presence. Use the appropriate gear and never assume the bear is unaware of your presence. It may be your last assumption and the bear's final mistake. By following a few simple rules and taking a common-sense approach to viewing and/or photographing wild bears, you become a role model for others, you protect the species you admire, and you have a better chance of walking out of the woods unharmed.

BIBLIOGRAPHY

Bryson, George. "The Final Days of Michio," *Anchorage Daily News*, We Alaskans, Anchorage, 1996.

Brown, Gary. *Great Bear Almanac*, Lyons & Bufford, New York, 1993.

Daren Fonda/Hamburg. "When Bears Get the Munchies," *Time*, September 2000.

Herrero, Stephen. *Bear Attacks: Their Causes and Avoidance*, Nick Lyons, New York, 1985.

McKibbon. "Polar Bear Kills One, Injures Two Others," *Nunatsiaq News*, Nortext Publishing Corporation (Iqaluit), July 1999.

Mueller & Reiss. "Tundra Terror," *Outdoor Life*, Times Mirror Magazines, Dec/Jan 2000.